The Evening and Morning Star
Volume 1, Numbers 1 & 2

By W. W. Phelps

ISBN: 978-1-63118-547-2

Mormon History Series

Other Books in this Series and Related Titles

Pearl of Great Price by Joseph Smith (978-1-63118-539-7)

The Angel of the Prairies or A Dream of the Future: Mormon History Series
By Elder Parley Parker Pratt (978-1-63118-541-0)

A Manuscript on Far West by Reed Peck (978-1-63118-544-1)

The Story of Mormonism by James E Talmage (978-1-63118-543-4)

An Address to All Believers in Christ Elder David Whitmer (978-1-63118-545-8)

The Philosophy of Mormonism by James E Talmage (978-1-63118-542-7)

The Book of Abraham: Mormon History by George Reynolds (978-1-63118-540-3)

The Testament of Abraham by Abraham (978-1-63118-441-3)

Private Diary of Joseph Smith 1832-1834 (978-1-63118-546-5)

The Evening and Morning Star Volume 1, Numbers 3 & 4 (978-1-63118-548-9)

The Evening and Morning Star Volume 1, Numbers 5 & 6 (978-1-63118-549-6)

The Evening and Morning Star Volume 1, Numbers 7 & 8 (978-1-63118-550-2)

The Evening and Morning Star Volume 1, Numbers 9 & 10 (978-1-63118-551-9)

The Evening and Morning Star Volume 1, Numbers 11 & 12 (978-1-63118-552-6)

The Testament of Moses by Moses (978-1-63118-440-6)

The Book of Parables by Enoch (978-1-63118-429-1)

The Secrets of Enoch by Enoch (978-1-63118-449-9)

American Indian Freemasonry by A C Parker (978-1-63118-460-4)

The Book of the Watchers by Enoch (978-1-63118-416-1)

Book of Dreams by Enoch (978-1-63118-437-6)

The Book of Astronomical Secrets by Enoch (978-1-63118-443-7)

Audio Versions are also available on Audible, Amazon and Apple

Other Books in this Series and Related Titles

The Hidden Mysteries of Christianity by Annie Besant (978–1–63118–534–2)

Rosicrucian Rules, Secret Signs, Codes and Symbols by various (978-1-63118-488-8)

History and Teachings of the Rosicrucians by W W Westcott &c (978-1-63118-487-1)

Freemasonry and the Egyptian Mysteries by C. W. Leadbeater (978-1-63118-456-7)

The Sepher Yetzirah and the Qabalah by M P Hall (978-1-63118-481-9)

The Psalms of Solomon by King Solomon (978-1-63118-439-0)

The Historic, Mythic and Mystic Christ by Annie Besant (978–1–63118–533–5)

Masonic and Rosicrucian History by M P Hall & H Voorhis (978-1-63118-486-4)

Some Deeper Aspects of Masonic Symbolism by A E Waite (978-1-63118-461-1)

Masonic Symbolism of King Solomon's Temple by A Mackey &c (978-1-63118-442-0)

The Old Past Master by Carl H Claudy (978-1-63118-464-2)

The Influence of Pythagoras on Freemasonry and Other Essays (978-1-63118-404-8)

The Mysteries of Freemasonry & the Druids by various (978-1-63118-444-4)

Masonic Symbolism of the Apron & the Altar by various (978-1-63118-428-4)

The Book of Wisdom of Solomon by King Solomon (978-1-63118-502-1)

Masonic Symbolism of Easter and the Christ in Masonry (978-1-63118-434-5)

The Odes of Solomon by King Solomon (978-1-63118-503-8)

Ancient Mysteries and Secret Societies by M P Hall (978-1-63118-410-9)

The Golden Verses of Pythagoras: Five Translations (978-1-63118-479-6)

Freemasonry & Catholicism by Max Heindel (978-1-63118-508-3)

A Few Masonic Sermons by A. C. Ward &c (978-1-63118-435-2)

Audio versions are also available on Audible, Amazon and Apple

Table of Contents

The Evening and the Morning Star

Volume 1

THE EVENING AND THE MORNING STAR.

Vol. I, Independence, Mo. June 1832, No. 1

Revelations.

THE ARTICLES AND COVENANTS OF THE CHURCH OF CHRIST.

The rise of the Church of Christ in these last days, being one thousand eight hundred and thirty years since the coming of our Lord and Savior Jesus Christ, in the flesh; it being regularly organized and established agreeable to the laws of our country, by the will and commandments of God in the fourth month and on the sixth day of the month, which is called April: Which commandments were given to Joseph, who was called of God and ordained an Apostle of Jesus Christ, an Elder of this Church; and also to Oliver, who was called of God an Apostle of Jesus Christ, an Elder of this Church; and ordained under his hand; and this according to the grace of our Lord and Savior Jesus Christ to whom be all glory both now and forever. Amen.

For, after that it truly was manifested unto this first Elder, that he had received a remission of his sins, he was entangled again in the vanities of the world, but after truly repenting God ministered unto him by an holy angel, whose countenance was as lightning, and whose garments were pure and white above all whiteness, and gave unto him commandments which inspired him from on high, and gave unto him power, by the means which were prepared, that he should translate a Book, which Book contained a record of a fallen people, and also the fulness [fullness] of the Gospel of Jesus Christ to the Gentiles; and also to the Jews, proving unto them, that the holy Scriptures are true; and also, that God doth inspire men and call them to his holy work, in these last days as well as in days of old, that he might be the same God forever. Amen.

Which Book was given by inspiration, and is called The Book of Mormon, and is confirmed to others by the ministering of angels, and declared unto the world by them: Wherefore, having so great witnesses, by them shall the world be judged, even as many as shall hereafter receive this work, either to faith and righteousness, or to the hardness of heart in unbelief, to their own condemnation, for the Lord God hath spoken it, for we, the Elders of the Church, have heard and bear witness to the words of the glorious Magesty [Majesty] on high; to whom be glory forever and ever. Amen.

Wherefore, by these things we know, that there is a God in Heaven, who is infinite and eternal, from everlasting to everlasting, the same unchangeable God, the maker of Heaven and earth and all things that in them is, and that he created man male and female, and after his own image, and in his own likeness created he them; and that he gave unto the children of men commandments, that they should love and serve him the only being whom they should worship, but by the transgression of these holy laws, man became sensual and devilish, and became fallen man: Wherefore the Almighty God gave his only begotten Son, as it is written in those Scriptures, which have been given of him, that he suffered temptations, but gave no heed unto them; that he was crucified, died, and rose again the third day, and that he ascended into heaven to sit down on the right hand of the Father, to reign with Almighty power, according to the will of the Father. Therefore, as many as would believe and were baptized in his holy name, and endured in faith to the end, should be saved; yea, even as many as were before he came in the flesh, from the beginning, who believed in the words of the holy Prophets, who were inspired by the gift of the Holy Ghost, which truly testified of him in all things, as well as those who should come after, who should believe in the gifts and callings of God, by the Holy Ghost, which beareth record of the Father and of the Son, which Father and Son and Holy Ghost, is one God, infinite and eternal, without end. Amen.

And we know, that all men must repent and believe on the name of Jesus Christ, and worship the Father in his name, and endure in faith on his name to the end, or they cannot be saved in the Kingdom of God: And we know, that Justification through the grace of our Lord and Savior Jesus Christ, is just and true; and we know, also, that Sanctification through the grace of our Lord and Savior

Jesus Christ, is just and true, to all those who love and serve God with all their mights, minds, and strength, but there is a possibility that men may fall from grace and depart from the living God. Therefore let the Church take heed and pray always, lest they fall into temptation; yea, and even he that is sanctified also: and we know, that these things are true and agreeable to the Revelation of John, neither adding to, nor diminishing from the prophecy of his Book; neither to the holy Scriptures; neither to the Revelations of God which shall come hereafter, by the gift and power of the Holy Ghost; neither by the voice of God; neither by the ministering of angels, and the Lord God hath spoken it; and honor, power, and glory be rendered to his holy name both now and ever. Amen.

And again, by way of commandments to the Church, concerning the manner of baptism: Behold whosoever humbleth himself before God and desireth to be baptized, and comes forth with a broken heart and a contrite spirit, and witnesseth unto the Church, that they have truly repented of all their sins and are willing to take upon them the name of Christ, having a determination to serve him unto the end, and truly manifest by their works that they have received the spirit of Christ unto the remission of their sins, then shall they be received unto baptism into the Church of Christ.

The duty of the Elders, Priests, Teachers, Deacons and members of the Church of Christ. An Apostle is an Elder, and it is his calling to baptize and to ordain other Elders, Priests, Teachers and Deacons, and to administer the flesh and blood of Christ according to the Scriptures, and to teach, expound, exhort, baptize, and watch over the Church, and to confirm the Church by the laying on of the hands and the giving of the Holy Ghost, and to take the lead of all meetings. The Elders are to conduct the meetings as they are led by the Holy Ghost. The Priests' duty is to preach, teach, expound, exhort and baptize, and administer the Sacrament, and visit the house of each member, and exhort them to pray vocally and in secret, and also to attend to all family duties; and ordain other Priests, Teachers, and Deacons, and take the lead in meetings; but none of these offices is he to do when there is an Elder present, but in all cases is to assist the Elder. The Teachers' duty is to watch over the Church always, and be with them, and strengthen them, and see that there is no iniquity in the Church, neither hardness with each other, neither lying nor back-biting nor evil speaking; and see that the Church meet together often, and also see that all the members do their duty; and he is to take the lead of meetings in the absence of the Elder or Priest, and is to be assisted always, and in all his duties in the Church by the Deacons; but neither the Teacher nor Deacons, have authority to baptize nor administer the Sacrament, but are to warn, expound, exhort and teach, and invite all to come unto Christ.

Every Elder, Priest, Teacher, or Deacon, is to be ordained according to the gifts and callings of God unto him, by the power of the Holy Ghost which is in the one who ordains him.

The several Elders composing this Church of Christ, are to meet in Conference once in three months, to do Church business whatsoever is necessary. And each Priest or Teacher, who is ordained by a Priest, is to take a cirtificate [certificate] from him at the time, which when presented to an Elder, he is to give him a License, which shall authorize him to perform the duty of his calling.

The duty of the members after they are received by baptism. The Elders or Priests are to have a sufficient time to expound all things concerning this Church of Christ to their understanding, previous to their partaking of the Sacrament, and being confirmed by the laying on of hands of the Elders; so that all things may be done in order. And the members shall manifest before the Church, and also before the Elders, by a godly walk and conversation, that they are worthy of it, that there may be works and faith agreeable to the holy Scriptures, walking in holiness before the Lord. Every member of this Church of Christ having children, is to bring them unto the Elders before the Church, who are to lay their hands on them in the name of the Lord, and bless them in the name of Christ. There cannot any one be received into this Church of Christ, who has not arrived to the years of accountability before God, and is not capable of repentance.

And baptism is to be administered in the following manner unto all those who repent: Whosoever being called of God and having authority given them of Jesus Christ, shall go down into the water with them, and shall say, calling them by name: Having authority given me of Jesus Christ, I baptize you in the name of the Father, and of the Son, and of the Holy Ghost. Amen. Then shall he immerse them in the water, and come forth again out of the water. And it is expedient that the Church meet together oft to partake of Bread and Wine, in remembrance of the Lord Jesus; and the Elder or Priest shall administer it, and after this manner shall he do, he shall kneel with the Church, and call upon the Father in mighty prayer saying: O God the Eternal Father, we ask thee in the name of thy Son Jesus Christ, to bless and sanctify this bread to the souls of all those who partake of it, that they may eat in remembrance of the body of thy Son, and witness unto thee, O God the Eternal Father, that they are willing to take upon them the name of thy Son, and always remember him, and keep his commandments which he hath given them, that they may always have his spirit to be with them. Amen. The manner of administering the Wine: Behold they shall take the Cup and say, O God, the Eternal Father, we ask thee in the name of thy Son Jesus Christ, to bless and sanctify this Wine to the souls of all those who drink of it, that they may do it in remembrance of the blood of thy Son, which was shed for them, that they may witness unto thee, O God the Eternal Father, that they do always remember him, that they may have his spirit to be with them. Amen.

Any member of this Church of Christ, transgressing or being overtaken in a fault, shall be dealt with according as the Scriptures direct. It shall be the duty of the several churches, composing this Church of Christ, to send one or more of their Teachers to attend the several Conferences, held by the Elders of this Church, with a list of the names of the several members, uniting themselves to the Church since the last Conference, or send by the hand of some Priest, so that there can be kept a regular list of all the names of the members of the whole Church, in a Book kept by one of the Elders; whosoever the other Elders shall appoint from time to time: and also, if any have been expelled from the Church, so that their names may be blotted out of the general Church Record of names. Any member removing from the Church where he resides, if going to a Church where he is not known, may take a letter certifying that he is a regular member and in good standing; which certificate may be signed by any Elder or Priest, if the member receiving the letter is personally acquainted with the Elder or Priest, or it may be signed by the Teachers or Deacons of the Church.

Behold, I say unto you, that all old Covenants have I caused to be done away in this thing, and this is a new and everlasting Covenant: even that which was from the beginning. Wherefore, although a man should be baptized an hundred times, it availeth him nothing, for ye cannot enter in at the straight gate by the law of Moses; neither by your dead works; for it is because of your dead works, that I have caused this last Covenant, and this Church to be built up unto me; even as in days of old. Wherefore, enter ye in at the gates as I have commanded, and seek not to counsel your God. Amen.

A PROPHECY GIVEN TO THE CHURCH OF CHRIST, MARCH 7, 1831.

HEARKEN, O ye people of my church to whom the Kingdom has been given: Hearken ye and give ear to him who laid the foundation of the earth; who made which live and move and have a being. And again I say, hearken unto my voice, lest death shall overtake you: in an hour when ye think not the summer shall be past, and the harvest ended, and your souls not saved. Listen to him who is the advocate with the Father, who is pleading your case before him; saying Father behold the sufferings and death of him who did no sin, in whom thou wast well pleased; behold the blood of thy Son which was shed, the blood of him whom thou gavest that thyself might be glorified; wherefore Father spare these my brethren that believe on my name, that they may come unto me and have everlasting life.

Hearken O ye people of my church, and ye Elders listen together, and hear my voice while it is called to-day and harden not your hearts; for verily I say unto you that I am Alpha and Omega, the beginning and the end, the light and the life of the world, a light that shineth in darkness and the darkness comprehendeth it not; I came unto my own and my own received me not; but unto as many as received me gave I power to do many miracles, and to become the sons of God, and even unto them that believed on my name gave I power to obtain eternal life. And even so I have sent mine everlasting covenant into the world, to be a light to the world, and to be a standard for my people and for the Gentiles to seek to it; and to be a messenger before my face to prepare the way before me. Wherefore come ye unto it, and with him that cometh I will reason as with men in days of old, and I will show unto you my strong reasoning; wherefore hearken ye together and let me show it unto you, even my wisdom, the wisdom of him whom ye say is the God of Enoch, and his brethren, who were separated from the earth, and were reserved unto myself, a city reserved until a day of righteousness shall come, a day which was sought for by all holy men, and they found it not because of wickedness and abominations, and confessed that they were strangers and pilgrims on the earth; but obtained a promise that they should find it, and see it in their flesh. Wherefore hearken and I will reason with you, and I will speak unto you and prophesy as unto me in days of old, and I will show it plainly as I showed it unto my disciples, as I stood before them in the flesh and spake unto them saying: As ye have asked of me concerning the signs of my coming, in the day when I shall come in my glory, in the clouds of Heaven, to fulfil [fulfill] the promises that I have made unto your fathers; for as ye have looked upon the long absence of your bodies to be a bondage, I will show unto you how the day of redemption shall come, and also the restoration of the scattered Israel.

And now ye behold this temple which is in Jerusalem, which ye call the house of God, and your enemies say that this house shall never fall. But verily I say unto you, that desolation shall come upon this generation as a thief in the night, and this people shall be destroyed and scattered among all nations, and this temple which ye now see, shall be thrown down that there shall not be left one stone upon another. And it shall come to pass, that this generation of Jews shall not pass away, until every desolation which I have told you concerning them, shall come to pass.

Ye say that ye know, that the end of the world cometh; ye say also that ye know, that the Heavens and the earth shall pass away; and in this ye say truly, for so it is; but these things which I have told you, shall not pass away until all shall be fulfilled. And this I have told you concerning Jerusalem, and when that day shall come, shall a remnant be scattered among all nations, but they shall be gathered again; but they shall remain until the times of the Gentiles be fulfiled [fulfilled]. And in that day shall be heard of wars and rumors of wars and the whole earth shall be in commotion, and men's hearts shall fail them, and they shall say that Christ delayeth his coming until the end of the earth. And the love of men shall wax cold, and iniquity shall abound; and when the time of the Gentiles is come in, a light shall break forth among them that sit in darkness, and it shall be in the fulness [fullness] of my Gospel; but they receive it not, for they perceive not the light, and they turn their hearts from me because of the precepts of men; and in that generation shall the times of the Gentiles be fulfilled: and there shall be men standing in that generation, that shall not pass until they shall see an overflowing scourge; for a desolating sickness shall cover the land; but my disciples shall stand in holy places and shall not be moved, but among the wicked, men shall lift up their voices and curse God and die; and there shall be earthquakes, also, in diverse places, and desolations, yet men will harden their hearts against me; and they will take up the sword one against another and they will kill one another: and now, when I the Lord had spoken these words unto my disciples, they were troubled, and I said unto them, be not troubled, for when all these things shall come to pass, ye may know that the promises which have been made unto you, shall be fulfilled, and when the light shall begin to break forth, it shall be with them like unto a parable which I will show you: ye look and behold the fig trees, and ye see them with your eyes, and ye say when they begin to shoot forth and their leaves are yet tender, ye say that summer is now nigh at hand; even so it shall be in that day, when they shall see all these things, then shall they know that the hour is nigh.

And it shall come to pass that he that feareth me shall be looking for the great day of the Lord to come, even for the signs of the coming of the son of man; and they shall see signs and wonders, for they shall be shown forth in the Heavens above and in the earth beneath; and they shall behold blood and fire, and vapors of smoke; and before the day of the Lord come the sun shall be darkened, and the moon be turned into blood, and stars fall from Heaven; and the remnant shall be gathered unto this place; and then they shall look for me, and behold I will come; and they shall see me in the clouds of Heaven, clothed with power and great glory, with all the holy angels; and he that watches not for me shall be cut off.

But before the arm of the Lord shall fall, an angel shall sound his trump, and the saints that have slept, shall come forth to meet me in the cloud. Wherefore if ye have slept in peace blessed are you, for as you now behold me and know that I am, even so shall ye come unto me and your souls shall live, and your redemption shall be perfected, and the saints shall come forth from the four quarters of the earth; then shall the arm of the Lord fall upon the nations, and then shall the Lord set his foot upon this mount, and it shall cleave in twain, and the earth shall tremble and reel to and fro, and the Heavens also shall shake and the Lord shall utter his voice and all the ends of the earth shall hear it, and the nations of the earth shall mourn, and they that have laughed shall see their folly, and calamity shall cover the mocker, and the scorner shall be consumed, and they that have watched for iniquity, shall be hewn down and cast into the fire.

And then shall the Jews look upon me, and say what are these wounds in thine hands, and in thy feet, then shall they know that I am the Lord; for I will say unto them, these wounds, are the wounds with which I was wounded in the house of my friends. I am he who was lifted up. I am Jesus that was crucified. I am the son of God. And then shall they weep because of their iniquities; then shall they lament because they persecuted their King. And then shall the heathen nations be redeemed, and they which knew no law shall have part in the first resurrection, and it shall be tolerable for them; and satan shall be bound that he shall have no place in the hearts of the children of men.

And at that day when I shall come in my glory, shall the parable be fulfilled which I spake concerning the ten virgins; for they that are wise and have received the truth and have taken the Holy Spirit for their guide, and have not been deceived; verily I say unto you, they shall not be hewn down and cast into the fire, but shall abide the day, and the earth shall be given unto them, for an inheritance; and they shall multiply and wax strong, and their children shall grow up without sin unto salvation, for the Lord shall be in their midst, and his glory shall be upon them, and he will be their King and their lawgiver.

And now, behold I say unto you, it shall not be given unto you to know any farther than this until the New Testament be translated, and in it all these things shall be made known; wherefore I give unto you that ye may now translate it, that ye may be prepared for the things to come; for verily I say unto you they are nigh even at your doors, and not many years hence ye shall hear of wars in your own lands. Wherefore I the Lord have said gather ye out from the eastern lands, assemble ye yourselves together ye Elders of my Church; go ye forth into the western countries, call upon the inhabitants to repent, and inasmuch as they do repent, build up churches unto me; and with one heart and with one mind, gather up your riches that ye may purchase an inheritance which shall hereafter be appointed unto you, and it shall be called the New Jerusalem, a land of peace, a city of refuge, a place of safety for the saints of the most high God; and the glory of the Lord shall be there, and the terror of the Lord also shall be there. And it shall come to pass, that the righteous shall be gathered out from among all nations, and shall come to Zion, singing with songs of everlasting joy, even so. Amen.

TO THE SAINTS OF CHRIST JESUS, SCATTERED ABROAD.

BRETHREN, As some of you have not been correctly informed, as we understand, respecting the order of the gathering of the saints to Zion: Therefore, for the benefit of the Church of Christ, generally, I subjoin a few extracts from the Revelation on this subject, that all may know and understand, and so conduct themselves, that order and not confusion may be produced; for God is a God of order.

In the love of Christ,

Yours. Edward .

EXTRACTS. "Let the privileges of the lands be made known from time to time by the Bishop, or the agent of the Church, and let the work of the gathering be not in haste, nor by flight, but let all be done as it shall be counselled [counseled] by the Elders of the Church, at the Conference, according to the knowledge which they receive from time to time." * * * * * * * * * "They who are privileged to go up unto Zion, let them carry up unto the Bishop, a certificate from three Elders of the Church, or a certificate from the Bishop, [in Ohio] otherwise he who shall go up unto the land of Zion, shall not be accounted a wise steward, or be accepted of the Bishop in Zion." * * * * * * * * * ** "Let those therefore who are among the Gentiles flee unto Zion, and let them who be of Judah flee unto Jerusalem." * * * * * * ** * "Go ye out from among the nations even from Babylon, from the midst of wickedness which is spiritual Babylon: but verily thus saith the Lord let not your flight be in haste, but let all things be prepared before you."

Selected.

THAT the world at large may the better judge, concerning the above prophecy, we add an extract from the Book of Mormon. It will be seen by this that the most plain parts of the New Testament, have been taken from it by the Mother of Harlots while it was confined in that Church,-say, from the year A. D. 460 to 1400: This is a sufficient reason for the Lord to give command to have it translated a new: Notwithstanding King James' translators did very well, all knowing that they had only the common faculties of men and literature, without the spirit of Revelation:-[Ed. E. & M. Star.]

And the angel of the Lord said unto me, Thou hast beheld that the Book proceeded forth from the mouth of a Jew; and when it proceeded forth from the mouth of a Jew, it contained the plainness of the Gospel of the Lord, of whom the twelve apostles bear record; and they bear record according to the truth which is in the Lamb of God; wherefore, these things go forth from the Jews in purity, unto the Gentiles, according to the truth which is in God; and after that they go forth by the hand of the twelve apostles of the Lamb, from the Jews unto the Gentiles; behold, after this, thou seest the foundation of a great and abominable church, which is the most abominable above all other churches; for behold, they have taken away from the Gospel of the Lamb, many parts which are plain and most precious; and also, many Covenants of the Lord have they taken away; and all this have they done, that they might pervert the right ways of the Lord; that they might blind the eyes and harden the hearts of the children of men; wherefore thou seest that after the Book hath gone forth through the hands of the great and abominable church, that there are mauy [many] plain and precious things taken away from the Book, which is the Book of the Lamb of God; and after that these plain and precious things were taken away, it goeth forth unto all the nations of the Gentiles; and after it goeth forth unto all the nations of the Gentiles; yea, even across the many waters which thou hast seen with the Gentiles which have gone forth out of captivity; and thou seest because of the many plain and precious things which have been taken out of the Book, which were plain unto the understanding of the children of men, according to the plainness which is in the Lamb of God; and because of these things which are taken away out of the Gospel of the Lamb, an exceeding great many do stumble, yea, insomuch [inasmuch] that Satan hath great power over them; nevertheless thou beholdest that the Gentiles which have gone forth out of captivity, and have been lifted up by the power of God above all other nations upon the face of the land, which is choice above all other lands, which is the land which the Lord God hath covenanted with thy father, that his seed should have, for the land of their inheritance; wherefore, thou seest that the Lord God will not suffer that the Gentiles will utterly destroy the mixture of thy seed, which is among thy brethren; neither will he suffer that the Gentiles shall destroy the seed of thy brethren; neither will the Lord God suffer that the Gentiles shall forever remain in that state of awful woundedness which thou beholdest that they are in, because of the plain and most precious parts of the Gospel of the Lamb which hath been kept back by the abominable church, whose formation thou hast seen; wherefore, saith the Lamb of God, I will be merciful unto the Gentiles, unto the visiting of the remnant of the House of Israel in great judgment.

And it came to pass that the angel of the Lord spake unto me, saying: Behold, saith the Lamb of God, after that I have visited the remnant of the House of Israel, and this remnant of which I speak, is the seed of thy father; wherefore, after that I have visited them in judgment, and smitten them by the hand of the Gentiles; and after that the Gentiles do stumble exceedingly, because of the most plain and precious parts of the Gospel of the Lamb which hath been kept back, by that abominable church, which is the mother of harlots, saith the Lamb; wherefore, I will be merciful unto the Gentiles in that day, saith the Lamb insomuch [inasmuch] that I will bring forth unto them in mine own power, much of my Gospel, which shall be plain and precious, saith the Lamb; for behold, saith the Lamb, I will manifest myself unto thy seed, that they shall write many things which I shall minister unto them, which shall be plain and precious; and after that thy seed shall be destroyed and dwindle in unbelief, and also, the seed of thy brethren; behold, these things shall be hid up, to come forth unto the Gentiles, by the gift and power of the Lamb; and in them shall be written my Gospel, saith the Lamb, and my rock and my salvation; and blessed are they which shall seek to bring forth my Zion at that day, for they shall have the gift and the power of the Holy Ghost; and if they endure unto the end, they shall be lifted up at the last day, and shall be saved in the everlasting kingdom of the Lamb; yea, whoso publish peace, that shall publish tidings of great joy, how beautiful upon the mountains shall they be.

PERSECUTION

THE following article has lately appeared in the news papers of the day, and we copy it to show that the religion of Jesus Christ, has always been persecuted. But when a saint lives to God, persecution or applause is all one: the soul is above them.

The first persecution of the Church of Christ under the Heathen Roman Emperors by Domitius Nero the VI., about the year 67, collected out of the lives of Nero, Caesar, Eusebius, and the Book of Martyrs. The occation [occasion] whereof was this, Nero having passed over the first five years of his reign somewhat plausibly, he then began to all manner of prodigious impieties; and among other designs, he had a great desire to consume the stately imperial city of Rome with fire; pronouncing king Pryamus a happy man, because he beheld the end of his kingdom and country together. Yea, said he, let not all be ruined, when I am dead, but while I am yet alive. And for effecting this villany [villainy], he sent divers to kindle the fires in sundry places; yea, some of his own bed chamber were seen to carry flax, tow, torches, &c. to farther it; and when any attempted to quench it, they were threatened for it. Others openly hurled fire brands: crying they knew what they did, there was one would bear them out. This fire began among the oil-men and druggists; the night watch and Pretorian [Praetorian] guards, did openly cherish it; and when it was thoroughly kindled, Nero went up to the top of Mecenes Tower, which overlooked the whole city, where he fed himself with the sight of the infinite burnings, and sang to his harp the burning of Troy.

Among other stately buildings that were burned down, the Circus or Race yard was one, being about half a mile in length, of an oval form, with rows of seats one above another, capable to receive at least a hundred and fifty thousand spectators, without uncivil shoulderings. But the particulars were innumerable, and the damage inestimable: besides which many thousands of people perished; the flame and smoke smothered some, the weight of ruins crushed others, the fire consumed others; others threw themselves into the fire, out of sorrow and despair, and villains slew many.

But Nero finding that this fire, which continued burning nine days, brought a great odium upon him. To excuse himself, he transferred the fault upon the Christians, as if out of malice, they had done it, and thereupon he raised this first persecution against them. For there was at this present a flourishing church of Christians, in Rome, even before St. Paul's arrival there, and Nero's own court was secretly garnished and enriched with some of those diamonds, whose salutations the apostle remembers in his Epistle to the Philippians [Philippians]. But while Nero with their blood, sought to quench and cover his own infamy, he procured himself new envy; while many that abhorred Christians for their religion, commiserated their sufferings as undeserved. Some he caused to be sewed up in skins of wild beasts, and then worried them to death with dogs; some he crucified, others he burnt in public, to furnish evening sports with bonfires. Many he caused to be packed up in paper stiffened in molten wax, with a coat of searcloth about their bodies and bound upwards to axletrees, many of which were pitched in the ground, and so set on fire at the bottom, to maintain light for Nero's night sports in his gardens. Some of them were gored in length upon stakes, the one end fastened in the earth, the other thrust into the fundaments, and coming out at their mouths.

Nor did the persecution rage in Rome alone, but it was extended generally over the whole empire, insomuch [inasmuch], that a man might then have seen cities lie full of dead mens' bodies, the old lying there together with the young; and the dead bodies of women cast out naked in the open streets, without any reference to their sex: Yea, his rage and malice was so great, that he endeavored to have rooted out the very name of Christians in all places. Whereupon Tertullian said, that it could be no ordinary goodness which Nero condemned: And, said he, we glory on the behalf of our sufferings, that they had such a dictator as he. But this persecution, like a blast, spread the religion that it blew, and having continued four years from the first rising, it expired in two most shining blazes, viz: in the martyrdom of the two great apostles, Peter and Paul; Peter was crucified with his head downwards, which manner of death himself made choice of; and while he thus hung upon the cross, he saw his wife going to her martyrdom, whereupon he much rejoiced; and calling her by name, he bade her remember the Lord Jesus Christ. At the same time, also Paul, before Nero, made a confession of his faith, and of the doctrines which he taught; whereupon he was condemned to be beheaded, and the emperor sent two of his esquires, Ferega and Parthemius, to bring him word of his death. They coming to Paul, heard him instruct the people, and thereupon desired him to pray for them, that they might believe; who told them, that shortly after, they should believe and be baptized. Then the soldiers led him out of the city to the place of execution, where he prayed, and so gave his neck to the sword and was beheaded. This was done in the fourteenth, which was the last year of Nero.

THE GREAT WALL OF CHINA.

"BUT the most stupendous work of this country is the great wall that divides it from N. Tartary. It is built exactly on the same plan as the wall of Pekin [Peking?], being a mount of earth cased on each side with brick or stone. [The astonishing magnitude of the fabric consists not so much in the plan of the work, as in the immense distance of fifteen hundred miles over which it is extended, over mountains of two and three thousand feet in height, across deep valleys and rivers.] The materials of all the dwelling houses of England and Scotland, supposing them to amount to one million eight hundred thousand, and to average on the whole, two thousand cubic feet of masonry or brick work, are barely equivalent to the bulk or solid contents of the great wall of China. Nor are projecting massy towers of stone and brick included in this calculation. These alone, supposing them to continue throughout at bow-shot distance, were calculated to cntain [contain] as much masonry and brick work as all London. To give another idea of the mass of matter in this stupendous fabric, it may be more than sufficient to surround the circumferenc [circumference] of the earth on two of its great circuits, with two walls each six feet high and two feet thick! It is to be understood, however, that in this calculation is included the earthy part in the middle of the wall."-[Barrow's Travels in China.]

EVIL communications corrupt good manners-saith the Scripture.

ON THE GOVERNMENT OF THE THOUGHTS.

IT is necessary that our thoughts should be under regular discipline, in order to the full and successful exertion of our mental powers. What is called a vigorous and active mind seems, after all, to mean only a mind, of which the thoughts are all subjected to the authority of its governing powers, and may therefore all be brought to bear, with their whole force, on the business in which it is occupied.-Attention seems only another name for that state of mind, when all its thoughts are fixed and collected and bent to a single point; and it is a power of attention, much more than any original and native diversity of talents, which constitutes the intellectual difference among men. Newton was accustomed to declare, that if he differed from his fellow men, he owed it to his power of patient meditation; in other words to his power of fixing his thoughts intently and long on any subject with which he was occupied. We must have all observed the truth of these remarks in the course of our various pursuits. If we examine our minds at those periods when they are most vigorously and successfully exerted, we shall observe that all other objects are excluded from our minds, and that our thoughts are concentrated and engrossed by the task in which we are employed. If on the contrary we observe ourselves when our minds are indisposed, reluctant and inefficient, we shall find that our dominion over our thoughts is lost, that attention is dissipated and distracted by a multitude of unrelated images; which float through the fancy, and that all our powers are weakened, because discordant and divided. The effect of suffering our thoughts to wander without guidance and without object is too obvious to have escaped the most careless observer. It breaks up all our habits of regular inquiry, indisposes us for any thing which requires seriousness and patience, and especially unfits us for meditation on divine things, which from their nature the mind is with so much difficulty brought steadily to contemplate. If then we desire to effect any thing valuable in this short life; if we seek to use our talents according to the purpose of the Giver; if we would improve our own minds for the service of

God, and the scenes of eternity; and contribute what we can, to the happiness and improvement of our fellow men, we must learn to control our thoughts, restrain our vain and wandering imaginations, and seek to make the proper business of life in our various callings, and the duties of devotion at their appointed seasons, fill and occupy our minds.

That our thoughts should be brought under discipline, is necessary, in the second place, for our happiness in actual life, and to fit us for its common scenes and duties. A great deal of misery is produced, particularly among those, who have no absorbing occupation, and those in whom the illusions of youth have not been corrected by the experience of actual life, by iudulging [indulging] the imagination in forming schemes and hopes of visionary felicity; or as it is sometimes called, "building castles in the air." It is indeed very delightful to give the reins to the thoughts, to send fancy on the wing from this world of imperfection and pain, and sorrow and sin, to scenes where every thing is perfect, happy, and fair; where nature wears an eternal bloom, where the skies are always blue, and the winds always balmy; where children are always virtuous, friends never faithless, and fortune is never fickle; where the eye knows no tear, and the heart no pang.

But this is not life as we must expect to find it. This is not the world in which we are to live, and in which we are to act. It is not intended that this state of trial should ever realize such dreams of fancy. And the effects of indulging this luxury of vain imagination are neither salutary nor innocent. If we could descend, indeed, from these airy fabrics of unreal felicity, and return as before to the common duties of life, the harshest epithet which we could apply to this employment would be, that it was useless. But both our happiness and our fitness for our duties are lessened by it. When we awake from these delusions, we feel the full force of the contrast between what we see and what we have imagined. The scenes and duties of common life appear tame and insipid, after gazing on the beautiful creations of fancy. The effects on the mind are precisely similar to those produced by works of fiction, except that in this case we read merely the fiction of another, and in that, we make the romance of ourselves; and are therefore more in danger of mistaking it for reality. The realities of life must always fall far short of the pictures of fancy. When we descend from the lofty regions where in imagination we have been dwelling, and are called on to perform the common-place duties of husbands and wives, and fathers, and children, and citizens, which the course can seldom call us to feel much either of rapture or of anguish, we miss the strong stimulus to which our passions have been accustomed. We find that we have been uourishing [nourishing] a sickly and fastidious delicacy, which revolts at the plain and homely, and sometimes coarse and disgusting employments, to which we are destined. A spirit of discontent and unhappiness is apt to spring up. We lose our cheerful acquiescence in the purpose of Providence, and our ready submission to that wisdom which always dicides [decide] best for us.

I do not say that this is always the effect of any degree of indulgence of these vain thoughts, but it is the tendency of it, and therefore it is that we must seek to banish them. We must refuse ourselves the luxury of solitary musing, and building castles in the air, and let hope and fancy and memory be regulated by reason and religion. Our expectations from life must become accommodated to its true state. We must be contented with the mixture of good and evil as it has been mingled for us, and not expect that we are born, with a peculiar destiny, to a happiness and perfection which is denied to others. If indeed it were nothing more than an unprofitable waste of time, that alone would be reason enough to confine this dissipation of thought, and restrain its irregularities. Enough surely of life is spent unprofitably, without giving any of the little, which remains, to the delusions of visionary happiness.

But the necessity of regulating our thoughts will appear more serious, when we consider their influence on our moral character. All action has its origin in the mind. The thought is the rudiment of the deed. Meditation produces desire, and desire leads to practice. If then we would have our actions rights, we must make our thoughts pure, and learn to forbear to think on what we are forbidden to do.

The manner in which evil thoughts are connected with bad actions is obvious. There is no one, who is yet innocent, who is not shocked by the idea of crimes, when they appear in all their magnitude and deformity. No one ever leaped over the limits of virtue, into the confines of confirmed vice, at a single bound. On the contrary, the exclamation, "Is thy servant a dog that he should do this thing," is the natural impulse of every man's mind, whose conscience is yet unseared, at the very suggestion of atrocious guilt. But by revolving with pleasure the safety, facility, or advantages, of a wicked deed, he finds his constancy waver, his resolution relax, his detestation soften. The idea of some fraudulent stratagem or scene of guilty pleasure, which at first perhaps was admitted into the mind from curiosity merely, is next regarded with complacency; comes at length to be cherished with fondness; at last assumes the form of desire; and how nearly allied is desire to transgression, there are too many of us, alas, who know! what we allow ourselves to which, we are soon induced to attempt to gain. He who suffers his thoughts and wishes to dwell too long on the pleasures and advantages which he should derive from what another possesses, will begin to reconcile his mind to some unlawful measure for procuring it. He, who suffers his imagination to be filled with images of guilty and degrading pleasure, will at length find his desire irresistibly stimulated to gratification. Every moment spent in meditation on sin increases its dangerous power over us, till at length the idea of pleasure overcomes the sense of guilt; the last limit of innocence is, though perhaps timidly and reluctantly, past-we enter into the confines of sin-it may be never to return.

We are thus irresistibly led to the conclusion, that he who would govern his actions by the laws of virtue, must regulate his thoughts by those of reason and religion. It is not possible that a man should walk outwardly in the law of God, who is constantly feeding his imagination with the pleasures of sin. The passions will at last act. It is difficult to stop when we have inflamed ourselves with every possible incentive to advance; to abstain when appetite is sharpened to its keenest edge.-Of what therefore we are forbidden to do, we must learn to forbid ourselves to think; and make the propriety of action a test of the propriety of thought. It if is wrong to gratify revenge, it is wrong to dwell on it in imagination. If we must resist all allurements of pleasure, we must refuse to contemplate them. We must not seek to indemnify ourselves for the restraints which we impose on our actions, by the sinful indulgences of imagination. There must be no discordance between the inward and outward man; thought, word, and deed, must constantly and inseparably unite.-[Thacher]

CULTIVATE THE MIND.

MAN was created to dress the earth, and to cultivate his mind, and glorify God. It, therefore, cannot be amis [amiss] for us, at this early period, to urge the disciples of our Lord, to study to shew [show] themselves approved in all things. For, when a disciple, educated, even as Paul at the feet of Gamaliel, is guided by the Holy Spirit, he not only edifies his fellow beings correctly, but he improves his faculties agreeable to the will of God. We select the following article from the Old Countryman, as worthy of a place under this head:-[Ed. E. &. M. Star.]

The venerable and Rev. Dr. Kidd, of Aberdeen, delivered the last Season, a Course of Lectures in Mechanic's Hall. Judging from the specimen before us, these Lectures must be invaluable to the general reader. We understand they have been printed.

In his introductory Lectures he said, in speaking of the advancement of knowledge: "Many a mechanic at the present day was a much greater adept in political economy than many legislators at the beginning of the present century and in the heart of England, where M'Culloch had lectured, they would find a journeyman mechanic rise up in any large assembly, and discuss the most abstruse points in this science, with such depth of thought, force and eloquence, that the orations of Pitt and Fox were fairly outshone. No man without careful observations would believe the march of mind which had taken place since the suicide, of Londonderry. Referring to the benefits of the cultivation of intellect, the Doctor said he might quote the beautiful passage of Dr. O.

Gregory, and ask what was Arkwright?-a barber. Ferguson?-a peasant. Herschell?-a pipe and tabor player. Watt?-a mathematical instrument maker. Brindly?-a mill wright. Nelson?-a cabin boy. Ramage?-a currier [courier].-These benefits exalted nations as well as individuals. What made William IV, the greatest monarch who now sat on a throne? Not the extent of his territories not his army, not his navy, but because he reigned over a free, educated, thinking and inquisitive people. Ignorance of their rights had once been cried up as the best way to make an obedient people; but the days were gone by for having the book of knowledge sealed, and education now ennobled the lowest in degree of the human race into men! Many a clown who stands in dumb and seemingly stupid gaze at the majesty of a full moon rising through a hazy horizon in an autumnal evening, or at the flash of the forked lightning, or at the fantastic shape of a transient cloud edged with gold by the gleams of a descending sun-who listen with ignorant but keen attention to the rolling thunder through the stupendous vault of the 'overhanging firmament,' or whistles as he returns from his daily task in sympathy with the minstrels of the grove, would-had he the benefit of education to brighten the rough diamond, and give scope 'to the genial current of the soul,' shine forth a Watt, or an Arkwright, in mechanics-a Washington or a Wellington in arms-a Nelson or a Cochrane on the wave-a Fox or a Canning in the cabinet-a Sheridan or a Mackintosh in the Senate-a Chalmers or a Thompson in the pulpit-a Jaffrey at the bar, or a Brougham on the woolsack."

The Doctor concluded in the following words:-"Most of you are as tall as me; most of you are as strong as me; all of you have as many bones and muscles as me; why is it that you are deficient in capacity?-because of your neglect in cultivating your minds and neglecting the means of raising yourselves by education."

THE TIMES IN WHICH WE LIVE.

WE have fallen upon other times than the church of God ever saw before; times in which the same amount of religious [religious] and moral influence which once availed to advance the cause of Christ will not enable it to hold its own. The intellect of man, wakened up to new activity, has burst the chains that bound it, and the barriers that confined it, and with ten-fold means of influence, is going forth in its mightsness [mightiness] to agitate society. Old foundations are broken, and principles and maxims are undergoing a thorough and perilous revision, and that too upon a mighty scale.

In our colonial state we were few, and poor and feeble. Intercourse was difficult and rare, and moral causes insulated and local. What was said in one colony was not heard in another, and what was done in one state was not felt in another. But now each colony is a state, and each state a nation, and intercourse is rapid, and local causes tall in their results throughout the whole, as every stroke on the body is felt through all the members. Nations compose our confederacy, and nations our religious denominations, and nations the army of the aliens.-[Spirit of the Pilgrims.]

It will be recollected that the reduction of duties on Teas, the second reduction on coffee, and the second reduction on salt, enacted by Congress in 1830, went into operation in Jan'y. The duty on coffee is now only one cent a pound-on salt, ten cents per bushel of 56 lbs.-on Teas from China, or any other place east of the Cape of Good Hope, in American vessles [vessels], as follows;

Bohea, 4 cts. per lb. Black, 10 cts. do. Green, 12 cts. do. Hyson and Y. Hyson, 18 cts. do. Imperial, Gun Powder and Gomee, 25 cts. do.

From any other place, or in vessels other than those of the United States.

Bohea, 6 cts. per lb. Black, 18 cts. do. Green, 20 cts. Hyson and Y. Hyson, 27 cts. do. Imperial, Gun Powder and Gomee, 37 cts do-[Jour. of Com.]

Mr. Geo. B. Raymond has returned from his mission to Holland relative to the jewels of the Princess of Orange. The value of the diamonds which he recovered on the Continent alone, were estimated to be worth L100,00. The Prince and Princess of Orange have written him a complimentary letter, accompanied by an elegant diamond ring and breast-pin. He has been very successful and dexterous in managing this affair; but in crossing the frontiers between Holland and Belgium, he was severely wounded by a horseman who cut his head open with a sabre [saber]-supposing him to be a spy.-[N. Y. Courier & Enquirer.]

The London Evangelical Magazine, for January, contains an address to the pastors and members of churches in the independent denomination, signed by George Redford and J. A. James, on the importance of a day of united prayer, in consequence of the fact, that "public affairs are in a state of extreme agitation; commerce and trade at a low ebb; the fatal pestilence, like a destroying angel, has set its foot upon our shores, and pauses only till the almighty Sovereign shall seal its commission; crimes, unexampled, have been brought to light; the church languishes; fanaticism and speculation, like a wrathful bolt from the skies, have scathed some of the ceders [cedars] of Lebanon," &c. &c. These are said to be distinct and imperative calls to humiliation and prayer.-[Christian Watchman.]

The following is found in an ancient History of Connecticut. Soon after the settlement of New-Haven; several persons went over to what is now the town of Milford, where, finding the soil very good, they were desirous to effect a settlement; but the premises were in the peaceable possession of the Indians, and some conscientious scruples arose as to the propriety of deposing and expelling them. To test the case a Church meeting was called, and the matter determined by the solemn vote of that sacred body. After several speeches had been made in relation to the subject, they proceeded to pass votes-the first was the following;-Voted, that the earth is the Lord's and the fullness thereof. This passed in the affirmative, and, "Voted, that the earth is given to the saints."-This was also determined like the former-mem. con.-3rd. "Voted, that we are the saints," which passed without a dissenting voice, the title was considered indisputable, and the Indians were soon compelled to evacuate the place and relinquish the possession to the rightful owners.

The public expenditures of England, during the year ending the 5th of January, 1832, were L. (?),123,298 2s. 11d. ($209,227,444) and the income L46,424,440 17s. 11 1/2 d. showing an excess of expenditure over income of L698,867 5s, 11 1/2 d.

A Mr. M'Farlane lately died in a mail stage in the western part of Pennsylvania. His pocket book was found to contain $8,000! We remark this to show the uniform practice which seems to prevail, of connecting every possible casualty, every mortal mischance with the subject of money. Does a man die, the question is asked, how much is he worth? Does he come to his end by drowning or in an apoplectic stroke, the bystanders immediately haul out his pocket-book and begin to count the cash it contains. The more money they find about his person, the more they wonder that he should die! A hundred dollars is thought to be a large sum for a mortal to carry about him; but $8,000 furnishes a subject of undying astonishment.-[Alb. Daily]

Extract of a letter dated Green Bay February 8:-The small pox is making dreadful ravages among the Indians along the western shore of lake Michigan. As many as sixty had died of this malady at Milwauky [Milwaukee], up to the last accounts.

The commerce of the west, dependent on the river Ohio and its tributary streams, gives employment to 190 steam boats. 5,000 flat boats and arks, and not less than 40,000 men and boys.

It appears by the report of the committee on the manufacture of salt, of the tariff convention, that the fixed capital in Ohio, used in making salt, amounts to $334, 762 and that the quantity of salt annually produced is 446,350 bushels. Four of the states make each a greater quantity than Ohio, viz: Massachusetts, New-York Pennsylvania and Virginia. The number of bushels annually made in the United States, is 4,444,929. Quantity imported, 5,901,175 bushels.

It has lately been discovered that the best paper for wrappers, writing, and printing, may be produced from wood shavings, boiled in mineral or vegetable, alkali. One hundred pounds of wood and twelve pounds of alkali will produce a ream of paper-[London paper.]

AWFUL AND ALARMING STATISTICS.

THE Rev. Dr. C. pastor of the Presbyterian church in York, Pa. has communicated in the Magazine of the German Reformed church, the result of an account kept during one year, of all the murders that came under his observation in reading various periodicals.-[Evang.]

The account has been kept for one year, commencing on the first day of January 1831, and to his surprise, the number amounts to 109, among which are some of, the most appalling kind, such as parents by their children, and children by their parents, husbands by their wives, and wives by their husbands, and several others of the most atrocious kind.

We are disposed to consider ourselves as moral, at least as the British nation and yet in the kingdom of England, whose population is about the same as ours, from a statistical account lately published, of all the crimes committed in that nation for 7 years, ending with that of 1830, the number of murders during that time is 103, averaging 15 each year, while ours amount to more than seven times that number.

As we cannot be supposed to be more wicked by nature than others, and as there is no other nation on earth where the inhabitants enjoy so abundantly, both necessaries and even comforts of life, and where there is less temptation for the commission of crimes, it becomes an important inquiry, how this awful increase of murder can be accounted for? Now we think, that it must occur to every serious and impartial observer, that of the 109 murders, a very large proportion was occasioned by the immoderate use of ardent spirits. This is truly an alarming fact, and ought to induce every one, who is a friend to religion and morality, to discourage as far as in his power the use of ardent spirits, which is the cause of many thousand deaths, every year in these United States.

Let even the temperate drinker ponder well, and consider what he is doing; for the greatest drunkard was once a temperate drinker, and could he have been foretold what crime he would one day commit, would have, perhaps, replied in the words of Hazael: "Is thy servant a dog that he should do this great thing?" Yet the crime has been committed, and several executions have taken place during the past year in consequence of it. It ought to be stated that the murders occasioned by the insurrection of the negroes in the southern states, are not included in the above, and there may also have been others in different parts of the United States that did not come under the observation of the subscriber.-Robert Cathcart.]

The more clearly the truth shines, the more will discordant parties, which are opposed to each other unite to oppose the progress of truth. Herod and Pilot though mortal enemies, united in persecuting Jesus Christ, and became friends in this work.

Whenever a society ceases to be virtuous, it flatters the world: For this reason the world persecutes true religion.

Native simplicity not unfrequently [infrequently] comprises beauty, virtue, and even the height of sublimity.

Sloth, like rust, consumes faster than labor wears, while the used key is always bright. Dost thou love life? Then do not squander time-for that is the stuff life is made of.

At the working man's house hunger looks in but never enters.

THE EVENING AND THE MORNING STAR

TO MAN

WITH the help of God, the first number of the Evening and the Morning Star, comes to the world for the objects specified in its prospectus, which was published last winter. That we should now recapitulate some of its leading objects, and briefly add a few remarks, will naturally be expected; and we cheerfully do so, that this generation may know, that the Star comes in these last days as the friend of man, to persuade him to turn to God and live, before the great and terrible day of the Lord sweeps the earth of its wickedness. That it comes not only as the messenger of truth, to bring the Revelations and Commandments of God which have been, but to publish those that God gives NOW, as in days of old, for he is the same God yesterday, to-day and forever; and is, after he was taken up, as mentioned in the first chapter of Acts, he through the Holy Ghost had given commandments unto the apostles whom he had chosen, what possible reason is there to suppose that he would neglect to do likewise NOW-before he comes in his glory; before he gathers his elect, (the house of Israel; see Isaiah 45:4). And even before John the Revelator must prophesy again before many peoples, and nations, and tongues, and kings? (see Rev. 10.) We know of no reason in the bible. That it comes as the harbinger of peace and good will to them that serve the Lord with a determination to have a part in the first Resurrection, and finally become kings and priests to God, the Father, in the celestial kingdom, where God, and Christ is, and where they will be for eternity; and where will be also, the general assembly of the first born, the Church of Enoch, who walked with God and built up Zion in the first days, which Zion and Enoch the Lord translated to paradise before the flood; but Isaiah says: Thy watchmen shall lift up the voice; with the voice together shall they sing: for they shall see eye to eye, when the Lord shall bring AGAIN ZION. That it comes according to the will of God, from those who are not ashamed to take upon them the name of Christ, and walk lowly in the valley of humiliation, and let the solemnities of eternity rest upon them: knowing that the great day of the Lord will soon usher in the Sabbath of creation, for the rest of the saints; that the Savior may reign his thousand years of peace upon the earth, while Satan is bound. That it comes in meekness and mercy to all mankind that they may do works meet for repentance and be saved in the first resurrection, and afterward dwell with the spirits of just men and made perfect in the celestial kingdom, which transcends the glory of the terrestrial as much as the terrestrial transcends the telestial, or the telestial transcends the prison of the imperfect. That it comes to bring good tidings of great joy to all people, but more especially the house of Israel scattered abroad, that the day of their redemption is near, for the Lord hath set his hand again the second time to restore them to the lands of their inheritance; ready to receive the Savior in the clouds of Heaven. That it comes to show that the ensign is now set up, unto which all nations shall come, and worship the Lord, the God of Jacob, acceptably. That it comes when war, and the plague or pestilence, as it is called, are sweeping their thousands and tens of thousands, to show that the days of tribulation, spoken of by our Savior, are nigh at hand, even at the doors. That it comes to repeat the great caution of Paul: Beware lest any spoil you, (the disciples of Christ,) through philosophy and vain deceit, after the tradition of men and the rudiments of the world. That it comes to prepare the way of the Lord, that when he comes he may have a holy people ready to receive him. That it comes to show that no man can be too good to be saved, but that many may be too bad. That it comes to declare that goodness consists in doing good, not merely in preaching it. That it comes to show that all men's religion is vain without charity. That it comes to open the way for Zion to arise and put on her beautiful garments and become the glory of the earth, that her land may be joined, or married, (according to the known translation of Isaiah,) to Jerusalem again, and they be one as they were in the days of Peleg. Thus it comes.

Man, being created but little below the angels, only wants to know for himself, and not by another, that, by obeying the commands of his Creator, he can rise again, after death, in the flesh, and reign with Christ a thousand years on the earth, without sin; be changed in the twinkling of an eye, and become a king and a priest to God in eternity-to forsake his sins, and say: Lord, I am thine! The first words of which we have account, that Jesus Christ, spake, concerning the things of eternal life, were: Suffer it to be so now: For thus it becometh us to fulfil [fulfill] all righteousness. Then he was baptized; and truly, if it became the Savior of the world, holy as he was, to be baptized in the meridian of time, to fulfil [fulfill] all righteousness, how much more necessary it is for man, to be baptized upon the very eve of the Sabbath of creation, to be saved? Let the heart answer the head, that the body may save the soul. As this paper is devoted to the great concerns of eternal things and the gathering of the saints, it will leave politics, the gainsaying of the world, and many other matters, for their proper channels, endeavoring by all means, to set an example before the world, which, when followed, will lead our fellow men to the gates of glory, where the wicked cease from troubling, and where the weary will find rest. That there may be errors both in us and in the paper, we readily admit, and we mean to grow better, till, from little children, we all come in the unity of the faith, and of the knowledge of the Son of God, unto a perfect man, unto the measure of the stature of the fulness [fullness] of Christ, which we pray may be the happy lot of thousands, before he comes with the hundred forty and four thousand that are without guile.

June, 1832. W. W. PHELPS.

TO THE CHURCH OF CHRIST ABROAD IN THE EARTH

IT is the duty of the Church of Christ, in Zion, to stand as an ensign to all nations, that the Lord hath set his hand the second time to restore the house of Israel to the lands of their inheritance &c; and it behooves the members of this Church, to manifest before the world by a godly walk; by a noble example, as well as by sterling precept; by prudence in living; by plainness in dress; by industry; by economy; by faith and works, and above all, by solemnity, humility and patience, that this is a day of warning and not a day of many words.

This being the order in Zion, how much more necessary is it, that the Churches of Christ, which have not yet come up to this land, should show the world, by well ordered conduct in all things, that they are the children of the living God? It is all-important and the salvation of many souls, depends upon their faultless example. They will, therefore, knowing that the Lord will suddenly come to his temple, do their part in preparing the way, by observing the Sabbath-day and keep it holy; by teaching their children the gospel, and learning them to pray; by avoiding extremes in all matters; by shunning every appearance of evil; by studying to be approved, and doing unto others, as they would have others do unto them; by bearing trouble and persecution patiently, without a murmur, knowing, that Michael, the arch angel, when contending with the devil, he disputed about the body of Moses, durst not bring against him a railing accusation, but said, The Lord rebuke thee. They will not only set an example worthy of imitation, but they will let their light so shine as that others, seeing, may go and do likewise. Example is the great thing that defies the world with all its vain glory; by letting their moderation be known unto all men, both in dress and in living; in words and in deeds; in watching and in praying; in love and in labor, and in works as well as in faith, they preach the world a lecture, they set the enquirer [inquirer] a sample, and teach all Christendom a lesson, that studied preaching and pulpit eloquence have failed to accomplish.

COMMON SCHOOLS.

THE disciples should loose [lose] no time in preparing schools for their children, that they may be taught as is pleasing unto the Lord, and brought up in the way of holiness. Those appointed to select and prepare books for the use of schools, will attend to that subject, as soon as more weighty matters are finished. But the parents and guardians, in the Church of Christ need not wait-it is all important that children, to become good should be taught so. Moses, while delivering the words of the Lord to the congregation of Israel, the parents, says, And these words which I command thee this day, shall be in thy heart: And thou shalt teach them diligently unto thy children, and shalt talk of them when thou sitest in thy house, and when thou walkest by the way, and when thou liest down, and when thou risest up. And thou shalt bind them for a sign upon thy hand, and they shall be as frontlets between thine eyes. If it were necessary then to teach their children diligently, how much more necessary it is now, when the Church of Christ is to be an ensign, yea, even a sample to the world, for good? A word to the wise ought to be sufficient, for children soon become men and women. Yes, they are they that must follow us, and perform the duties which, not only appertain to this world, but to the second coming of the Savior, even preparing for the Sabbath of creation, and for eternity.

THE BOOK OF MORMON.

THERE are not a few honest enquiring [inquiring] persons, who wish to learn the truth of the Book of Mormon. To put them in possession of such testimony as may lead to truth, is our duty, and, after stating that this Book contains a record of that branch of the tribe of Joseph which was separated from his brethren, according to the 49th chapter of Genesis, we say read the 37th chapter of Ezekiel and if the STICK OF EPHRAIM, therein mentioned does not mean the Book of Mormon, what does it mean? Isaiah has information, which, if rightly understood, ought to wake the world; the Lord says he will proceed to do a marvelous work among this people, a marvelous work and a wonder, and who dare dispute the Lord?

Independent of Bible proof on the subject before us, we have the remains of towns, cities, forts &c., which silently declare to the beholder: We were built by a civilized people.

As man cannot trust in man, we request all that wish the truth on this great subject, to enquire [inquire] of the Lord, who will always answer the pure in heart.

TO AGENTS AND THE PUBLIC.

EVERY person that will procure ten subscribers for the Star, and transmit to us, free of postage, $10, (U. S. paper,) shall be entitled to a paper per. an. gratis. In all cases, payment must be made to us through the post office, or to an authorized agent, before the Star will be forwarded.

(->) As the public seem somewhat astonished, that we, among all the light of this century, should have "sacred records which have slept for ages" to publish, it is our duty to say, that we shall take an extract from The Prophecy of Enoch, for our second or third number. Jude spake of this prophet in the 14th verse of his epistle. There are too many books mentioned and missing in the Bible, for any one to query about more sacred records.

(->) THE Star-office is situated within 12 miles of the west line of the state of Missouri:-which at present, is the western limits of the United States, and about 120 miles west of any press in the state- In about 39 degrees of North Latitude, and about 17 1/2 degrees of West Longitude; 2 1/2 miles south of Missouri River; 280 miles by land, or 500 by water west of St. Louis; nearly 1200 west of Washington; 1300 from New-York, and more than 1500 from Boston.

(->) EARLY in May, Capt. Bonaville's Company, (150) under the command of Capt. Walker passed this town, on its way to the Rocky Mountains, to trap and hunt for fur in the vast country of the Black Feet Indians. About the middle of May, Capt. Soublett's Company, (70) passed, for the Rocky Mountains, on the same business. At which time, also, Capt. Wythe of Mass., with a Company of 30, passed for the mouth of Oregon River, to prepare (as it is said) for settling a territory. During the month of May there also passed one Company bound to Santa Fee.

About the 8th or 9th of this month Capt. Blackwell's Company, (60 or 70) passed this place for the Rocky Mountains, in addition.

(->) UNDER the head of SELECTIONS, we intend to furnish the disciples with well-written articles from celebrated authors, that they may be enabled to judge between right and wrong; between the church of Christ and the church of man, and set an example worthy of imitation.

Under the head, also, of WORLDLY MATTERS, shall be given, as far as our limits may permit, such items of general news, as may enable the saints to know the condition of the world. We, therefore, cannot be responsible for the errors that may be in the article or items, but shall endeavor, at all times, to give correct information, praying to God continually for his spirit to guide us to all truth.

NEWS.

UNDER this head in addition to Worldly Matters on an other page, we shall furnish such items as may interest the public. We begin by stating, that on the 4th inst. A Mr. Taylor was stabbed to death by A Mr. Socie at Lexington, Mo. Socie is in Jail.

A large six story store in New-York, fell upon its inmates, not long since, and crushed several of them to death. A late arrival from Colombia, states that war has been declared between the place and New Grenada. We learn from Mr. Joseph Sterett, supercargo of the brig Brazen, arrived at this port yesterday from Ponce, Porto [Puerto] Rico, that the town of Guayanna [Guyana], in that island, was entirely consumed by fire about the 11th of April. The light was distinctly seen at Ponce.-Letters detailing the event were received at the latter place which stated that the warehouses on the beach were injured. The brig Pedlar had sailed from Ponce with a cargo of lumber for the relief of the sufferers.-[Amer.] The steam boats Brandywine, Talisman, and Dolphin, were burnt this spring; some others have been sunk, damaged or injured, we believe, which brings the unwelcome tidings of some deaths. Mina has been found guilty of the murder of Mr. Chapman, at Doyalstown, Pa. It is said that the East India company, in 1668, imported 100-lbs of good tea. In 1830, about 63,000,000!! A treaty has been concluded between our government and the Wyandots, for the cession of 16,000 acres of land in Ohio, at $1,25 per acre. Robert Dale Owen, the free thinker, who was in favor of free intercourse independent of matrimony, has lately been married.

INDIAN WAR.-Reports have reached us of disturbances having broken out between the Indians, and the frontiers of Illinois. The Indians are undoubtedly the aggressors, and it is said they have murdered several men, women, and children, and made some captives. General Atkinson, and General Whitesides, with a considerable detachment of troops, are already in pursuit of the Indians; these troops in connection with 2,000 Militia of the state, which are called out by Gov. Reynolds, must quiet them as well as the fears of the public. There are but a handful of Indians at any rate, and the United States are strong enough to crush them at one step. In addition, we understand, the Otto passed our landing not long since, for a part of the troops stationed at Cantonment Leavenworth.-[Ed. E. & M. Star.]

The following account of a natural Phenomenon is from the Cosmopolitan, a paper published in Buenos Ayres [Aires], dated on the 15th. ult. On Saturday last between one and two o'clock, a dense black cloud was observed approaching from the westward. The haste and apparent terror of street passengers at the time, indicated to us the nature of the coming storm, and we turned to behold an object most terrifically sublime. The cloud at first resembled black smoke rolling onwards with indescribable rapidity, driving before it affrighted birds screaming in terror at seeming approaching destruction. In a moment it was over our heads-the sun was hid from us-we were in darkness-utter darkness. We stood before an open window, but, for the space of nearly a minute, could not perceive that it was one. Then was heard a loud peal of thunder, which was immediately succeeded by a shower of "mud" thick mud,- "and there was light"-the dark veil which enveloped us had been wrent, a part falling to the earth; mingled with water. On the reappearance of light, surrounding objects presented themselves in a different color. The fronts of houses which, but a moment before, appeared to our view white as snow, now were a dingy robe. We conversed yesterday with a gentleman just from San Pedro, who states that in the neighborhood of that place there has lately been plentiful rains; and that the lakes are well filled, the cattle, however, had all strayed from Estancias, during the drought, in pursuit of water; but the owners entertained a hope that part of them would return.

CRIMES IN ENGLAND-An official return has appeared, giving details of the number of persons apprehended by the New Poliece [Police] during the last year. It is true the larger portion were taken up for crimes of minor magnitude; but the whole number reaches a fearful amount, comprising 45,907 males, forming a grand total of no less than 72,824 persons, all of whom have been thus dragged through the hands of justice. Out of this number, committed to take their trial is only 2,955, viz.-2,272 males, and 673 females-including 2,279 for larceny, 227 for picking pockets, and many for minor offences [offenses]; thus leaving, we are happy to say, cmparatively [comparatively] few charged with the heavier crimes-21,843, two-thirds of that number, being males, were summarily convicted by the different Police Magistrates: 24,239 were discharged by the same-while no less a number than 23,787 persons stated to be drunken cases, comprising 14,328 males, and 9,349 females, were apprehended determined in the different police quarters for more or less time, and discharged by the respective Superintendents.

FOREIGN NEWS.

WE select an item or two of foreign news, to give the reader an idea of the world, and its agitations [agitation's] at the present day. We would here remark, in giving the News of the world, we take it as we find it, and will not be responsible for its truth.

PORTUGAL. Our Madrid and Lisbon letters continue to strengthen the impression that, in the approaching struggle between the brothers for the Crown of Portugal, Spain will act neutrally. The latest accounts from Don Pedro state that he took possession of St. Michael's on the 22d, amid the congratulations of the inhabitants; and an expedition under Admiral Sartorios, was to sail against Maderia upon the 26th, which, it was confidently expected, would also succeed in that important island to the lawful Sovreign [Sovereign] of Portugal. The intelligence from Lisbon itself is satisfactory-for Don Miguel, though strong in all the material of defence [defense], was becoming more weak in the fidelity of his troops. Even the tyrant himself, since the refusal which he had met with from Spain, is said to be desponding as to the issue of the coming conflict. The confidence of Don Pedro's friends remained unabated.

IRELAND. Two poor creatures died last week of starvation in the streets of Dublin. Irish poor.-Mr. Sadler has given notice that, on the 10th of May he will apply for leave to bring in a bill "for establishing a permanent provision for the suffering and destitute poor of Ireland, by levy upon real property of that part of the United Kingdom, and more particularly upon that of the absentees.

FRANCE. It is impossible any longer to doubt that there is an organized band in Paris, who poison the wine, the milk and the water, throughout the city and the environs. The people are greatly exasperated, the citizens are in a perfect dread, and cry loudly against so infernal a conspiracy.

THE CHOLERA MORBUS.

IT is with no ordinary feelings, that we select an item or two, in relation to the Cholera Morbus. Its ravages, for the past year, on the Eastern Continent, have been great, so that, if ever the pestilence walked in darkness, or destruction wasted at noon day, now is the time, but the Lord hath declared that it should be so before he came in his glory, and we have only to rely on him for deliverance, when he sweeps the earth with the besom of destruction.-[Ed. Eve. & Morn. Star.]

According to late accounts from the frontiers of Persia, the plague and cholera had hardly begun to subside in that country. In some provinces those formidable diseases had carried off more than 2-3d of the population. The province of Ghillan appeared to have been among the greatest sufferers. Out of a population of 300,000 only 60,000 men and 44,000 Women and children remained. The eggs of the silk-worms have been completely destroyed there, and it was calculated that it would take seven years to produce the same quantity of worms as formerly. Before the arrival of these diseases, the revenue of Ghillan were usually framed at 350,000 tomauns. Since then, no more than 80,000 tomauns could be obtained.

In the East the Cholera frequently falls upon a community like a shower of grape shot. It was decided in the King of Siam's council, on a visitation of this kind, that it might be caused by a monster, who might be scared from the coast by making a terrific noise. His Majesty, in consequence, moved out against the invisible enemy, at the head of 30,000 subjects, all on the stretch to produce sounds of horror. He lost 5,000 in one day; and returned vanquished. A Persian writer says; "We were apprized [apprised] that the cholera was at Shiraz, by finding one morning when we awoke, that it had carried off two thousand inhabitants during the night." [London Medical Journal.]

Cholera in France. Ten persons have already been removed to the Hotel Dieu where preparations are made for the reception of many more. Seven persons died, of it yesterday; among whom was the cook of Marshal Lobau. The autopsy of five bodies took place in the presence of 38 medical men and of the Minister of the Public Works, M. d'Argout, by whom no doubt is entertained of the existence of the malady.

The Government, in order to prevent the extension of the alarm necessarily consequent on the report, endeavoured [endeavored] this morning to contradict it, but contradiction was useless. The medical board has been assembled, in order to make all proper regulations.

April 3.-The cholera is increasing in a dreadful manner. The official report states, that since Sunday at one o'clock, up to yesterday, there had been 735 cases, and 267 deaths, principally among the lower class. The King, & the whole of the Royal Family, with their usual benevolence, have sent a donation of 100,000 francs (L4000,) to be applied for the alleviation of the sufferings of the poor, and each of the Ministers have sent a donation of 1000 francs. The troops are all in good health. The cholera has manifested itself at Calais, Etampee, Orleans, and other towns. A letter from Calais, dated March 31, says: "The cholera morbus has been at Calais for the last two days, and several individuals have already died from it. It has been remarked that the disorder principally attacks the persons living in habits of filth and drunkenness.

The Cholera is in Ireland and England. The amount of deaths by it, in London, for the last week of March, was towards 1000.

To give the reader, a sketch of the above calamity, as well as other common news, is, under the peculiar situation in which we stand before the world, all that we shall aim at: and it might not be amiss for all candid readers, to make some allowances for the agitation of the times, when they read what we publish.-The present age is big with events that concern the world, and we only add: WATCH.

HYMNS

Selected and prepared for the Church of Christ, in the last days.

What fair one is this, in the wilderness trav'ling, A blessing a blessing, the Savior is coming,

Looking for Christ, the belov'd of her heart? As prophets and pilgrims of old have declar'd;

O this is the Church, the fair bride of the Savior, And Israel, the favor'd of God, is beginning

Which with every idol is willing to part. To come to the feast for the righteous prepar'd.

While men in contention, are constantly howling, In the desert are fountains continually springing,

And Babylon's bells are continually tolling, The heavenly music of Zion is ringing;

As though all the craft of her merchants was failing, The saints all their tithes and offerings are bringing;

And Jesus was coming to reign on the earth. They thus prove the Lord and his blessing receive.

There is a sweet sound in the gospel of heaven, The name of Jehovah is worthy of praising,

And people are joyful when they understand; And so is the Savior an excellent theme:

The saints on their way home to glory, are even The Elders of Israel a standard are raising,

Determin'd, by goodness, to reach the blest land. And call on all nations to come to the same:

Old formal professers [professors] are crying "delusion," These Elders go forth and the gospel are preaching,

And high minded hypocrites day, "'tis confusion," And all that will hear them, they freely are teaching,

While grace is pour'd out in a blessed effusion, And thus is the vision of Daniel fulfilling [fulfilling];

And saints are rejoicing to see priest-craft fall. The Stone of the mountains will soon fill the earth.

-oOo-

GLORIOUS things of thee are spoken, Who can faint, while such a river, Bless'd inhabitants of Zion,

Zion, city of our God! Ever flows their thirst t'assuage? Purchas'd with the Savior's blood!

He whose word cannot be broken, Grace which like the Lord, the giver, Jesus whom their souls rely on,

Chose thee for his own abode: Never fails from age to age. Makes them kings and priests to God.

On the Rock of Enoch founded; Round each habitation hov'ring, While in love his people raises,

What can shake thy sure repose? See the cloud and fire appear! With himself to reign as kings;

With Salvation's walls surrounded, For a glory and a cov'ring, All, as priests, his solemn praises,

Thou may'st smile on all thy foes. Showing that the Lord is near: Each for a thank-offering brings.

See the stream of living waters, Thus deriving from their banner, Savior, since of Zion's city

Springing from Celestial love, Light by night and shade by day; I through grace a member am;

Well supply thy sons and daughters, Sweetly they enjoy the spirit, Though the world despise and pity,

And all fear of drought remove; Which he gives them when they pray. I will glory in thy name;

Fading are all worldly treasures,

With their boasted pomp and show!

Heav'nly joys and lasting pleasures

None but Zion's children know.

-oOo-

THE time is nigh, that happy time, In one sweet symphony of praise,

That great, expected, blessed day, The Jews and Gentiles will unite;

When countless thousands of our race, And infidelity, o'er come,

Shall dwell with Christ and him obey. Return again to endless night.

The prophecies must be fulfil'd From east to west, from north to south,

Though earth and hell should dare oppose; The Savior's Kingdom shall extend,

The stone out of the mountain cut, And every man in every place,

Though unobserved, a Kingdom grows. Shall meet a brother and a friend.

Soon shall the blended Image fall,

Brass, silver, iron, gold and clay;

And superstition's dreadful reign,

To light and liberty give way.

-oOo-

REDEEMER of Israel, How long we have wandered

Our only delight, As strangers in sin,

On whom for a blessing we call; And cried in the desert for thee!

Our shadow by day, Our foes have rejoic'd

And our pillar by night, When our sorrows they've seen

Our king, our companion, and all. But Israel will shortly be free.

We know he is coming As children of Zion

To gather his sheep, Good tidings for us:

And plant them in Zion, in love, The tokens already appear;

For why in the valley Fear not and be just,

Of death should they weep, For the Kingdom is ours,

Or alone in the wilderness rove? And the hour of Redemption is near.

The secret of Heaven,

The myst'ry below,

That many have sought for so long,

We know that we know,

For the spirit of Christ,

Tells his servants they cannot be wrong.

-oOo-

ON mountain tops the mount of God The rays that shine from Zion's hill, No war shall rage, no hostile band

In latter days, shall rise Shall lighten every land; Disturb those peaceful years;

Above the summit of the hills, Her King shall reign a thousand years, To ploughshare [plowshare] men shall beat their swords,

And draw the wond'ring eyes. And all the world command. To pruning-hooks their spears.

To this the joyful nations round, Among the nations he shall judge, Come then, O house of Jacob, come,

All tribes and tongues shall flow; His judgments truth shall guide; And worship at his shrine;

Up to the mount of God, they'll say, His sceptre [scepter] shall protect the meek, And, walking in the light of God,

And to his house we'll go. And crush the wicked's pride. With holy beauties shine.

[THE PRAYER OF A WISE HEATHEN.]

GREAT JOVE, this one petition grant;

(Thou knowest best what mortals want;)

Ask'd or unask'd, what's good supply;

What's evil, to our pray'rs deny!

-oOo-

The body is but chaff- Come saints and drop a tear or two, The rising Lord forsook the tomb,

The soul may live in glory, For him who groan'd beneath your load; (In vain the tomb forbid his rise,)

When this Earth's epitaph He shed a thousand drops for you Cherubic legions guard him home,

Is written in its ashes! A thousand drops of precious blood. And shout him welcome to the skies.

HE died! the great Redeemer died! Here's love and grief beyond degree; Wipe off your tears, ye saints, and tell

And Israel's daughters wept around; The Lord of glory died for men! How high your great deliv'rer reigns:

A solemn darkness veil'd the sky; But lo! what sudden joys were heard, Sing how he triumph'd over hell,

A sudden trembling shook the ground! Jesus though dead's reviv'd again! To bind the Dragon fast in chains!

Say, "Live for ever wond'rous King!

Born to redeem and strong to save!"

Then ask the monster-"Where's thy sting?

And where's thy vict'ry boasting grave?"

-oOo-

[From the Book of Mormon]

HEARKEN, O ye Gentiles, and hear the words of Jesus Christ, the Son of the living God, which he has commanded me that I should speak concerning you: for behold he commandeth me that I should write, saying, Turn all ye Gentiles from your wicked ways, and repent of all your evil doings, of your lyings and deceivings, and of your whoredoms, and of your secret abominations and your idolatries, and of your murders, and your priestcrafts, and your envyings, and your strifes, and from all your wickedness and abominations, and come unto me, and be baptized in my name, that ye may receive a remission of your sins, and be filled with the Holy Ghost, that ye may be numbered with my people, which are of the house of Israel.

BE always so precisely true, in whatsoever thou relatest of thy own knowledge that thou mayest get an undoubted and settled reputation of veracity; and thou wilt have this advantage, that every body will believe (without farther proof) whatsoever thou affirmest, be it never so strange.

Be a most strict observer of order, method and neatness, in all thy affairs and management. Saturday concludes the week; if thou wouldest set apart that day, take a view of all thy concerns, to note down what is wanting, and to put every thing into its place, thou-wouldest prevent much troublesome confusion, and save abundance of vexation and pains.-[U. S. Gaz.]

THE EVENING AND THE MORNING STAR IS PUBLISHED EVERY MONTH AT INDEPENDENCE, JACKSON COUNTY, MO., BY W. W. PHELPS & CO.

THE PRICE IS ONE DOLLAR FOR A YEAR IN ADVANCE, EXCEPT SPECIAL CONTRACTS WITH THE CHURCH.

EVERY PERSON THAT SENDS US $10, (U. S. PAPER,) SHALL BE ENTITLED TO A PAPER FOR A YEAR, GRATIS. ALL LETTERS TO THE EDITOR, OR PUBLISHERS, MUST BE POST PAID.

(->) ADVERTISEMENTS WILL BE INSERTED TO ORDER, IN A SUPPLEMENT,

AT THE USUAL RATES.

PRINTING, OF MOST KINDS, DONE TO ORDER, AND IN STYLE.

THE EVENING AND THE MORNING STAR

Vol. I, INDEPENDENCE, MO. JULY, 1832. No. 2.

Revelations.

EXTRACT FROM THE LAWS FOR THE GOVERNMENT OF THE CHURCH OF CHRIST

AGAIN I say unto you, that it shall not be given to any one to go forth to preach my gospel, or to build up my church, except he be ordained by some one who has authority, and it is known to the church that he has authority, and has been regularly ordained by the hands of the church. And again, the elders, priests, and teachers of this church, shall teach the Scriptures which are in the Bible, and the Book of Mormon, in the which is the fulness [fullness] of the Gospel; and they shall observe the Covenants and church Articles to do them; and this shall be their teachings. And they shall be directed by the Spirit, which shall be given them by the prayer of faith; and if they receive not the Spirit, they shall not teach. And all this they shall observe to do, as I have commanded concerning their teachings, until the fulness [fullness] of my Scriptures are given. And as they shall lift up their voices by the Comforter, they shall speak and prophesy as seemeth me good; for behold, the Comforter knoweth all things, and beareth record of the Father, and of the Son.

And now behold, I speak unto the church: Thou shalt not kill; and he that killeth, shall not have forgiveness, neither in this world, nor in the world to come. And again, thou shalt not kill; he that killeth shall die. Thou shalt not steal; and he that stealeth and will not repent, shall be cast out. Thou shalt not lie; he that lieth and will not repent, shall be cast out. Thou shalt love thy wife with all thy heart, and shall cleave unto her and none else; and he that looketh upon a women [woman?] to lust after her, shall deny the faith, and shall not have the Spirit; and if he repent not, he shall be cast out. Thou shalt not commit adultery; and he that commiteth adultery and repenteth not, shall be cast out; and he that commiteth adultery and repenteth with all his heart, and forsaketh and doeth it no more, thou shalt forgive him; but if he doeth it again, he shall not be forgiven, but shall be cast out. Thou shalt not speak evil of thy neighbor, or do him any harm. Thou knowest my laws, they are given in my Scriptures, he that sinneth and repenteth not, shall be cast out.

If thou lovest me, thou shalt serve me and keep all my commandments; and behold, thou shalt consecrate all thy properties, that which thou hast unto me, with a covenant and a deed which cannot be broken; and they shall be laid before the bishop of my church, and two of the elders, such as he shall appoint and set apart for that purpose. And it shall come to pass, that the bishop of my church, after that he has received the properties of my church, that it cannot be taken from the church, he shall appoint every man a steward over his own property, or that which he has received, inasmuch as shall be sufficient for himself and family; and the residue shall be kept to administer to him who has not, that every man may receive according as he stands in need; and the residue shall be kept in my storehouse, to administer to the poor and needy, as shall be appointed by the elders of the church and the bishop; and for the purpose of purchasing lands, and the building up of the New Jerusalem, which is hereafter to be revealed; that my covenant people may be gathered in one, in the day that I shall come to my temple: And this I do for the salvation of my people. And it shall come to pass, that he that sinneth and repenteth not shall be cast out, and shall not receive again that which he had consecrated unto me: For it shall come to pass, that which I spake by the mouths of my prophets shall be fulfilled; for I will consecrate the riches of the Gentiles, unto my people which are of the house of Israel. And again, thou shalt not be proud in thy heart; let all thy garments be plain, and their beauty the beauty of the work of thine own hands, and let all things be done in cleanliness before me.

Thou shalt not be idle; for he that is idle shall not eat the bread, nor wear the garments of the laborer. And whosoever among you that are sick, and have not faith to be healed, but believeth, shall be nourished in all tenderness with herbs and mild food, and that not of the world; and the elders of the church, two or more shall be called, and shall pray for, and lay their hands upon them in my name, and if they die, they shall die unto me; and if they live, they shall live unto me.-Thou shalt live together in love, insomuch that thou shalt weep for the loss of them that die, and more especially for those that have not hope of a glorious resurrection. And it shall come to pass, that those that die in me shall not taste of death, for it shall be sweet unto them; and they that die not in me, wo unto them; for their death is bitter. And again, it shall come to pass, that he that has faith in me to be healed, and is not appointed unto death, shall be healed. He who has faith to see, shall see; he who has faith to hear, shall hear; the lame who have faith to leap shall leap; and they who have not faith to do these things, but believe in me, have power to become my sons, and inasmuch as they break not my laws, thou shalt bear their infirmities. Thou shalt stand in the place of thy stewardship: Thou shalt not take thy brother's garment; thou shalt pay for that which thou shalt receive of thy brother. And if thou obtainest more than that which would be for thy support, thou shalt give it into my storehouse, that all things may be done according to that which I have spoken. Thou shalt ask and my Scriptures shall be given as I have appointed; and for thy safety it is expedient that thou shalt hold thy peace concerning them, until ye have received them; then I give unto you a commandment that ye shall teach them unto all men; and they also shall be taught unto all nations, kindreds, tongue and people.

Thou shalt take the things which thou hast received, which thou knowest to have been my law, to be my law, to govern my church; and he that doeth according to these things shall be saved, and he that doeth them not shall be damned, if he continue. If thou shalt ask, thou shalt receive revelation upon revelation, knowledge upon knowledge, that thou mayest know the mysteries, and the peaceable things of the kingdom; that which bringeth joy, that which bringeth life eternal. Thou shalt ask and it shall be revealed unto you in my own due time where the New Jerusalem shall be built. And behold, it shall come to pass, that my servants shall be sent both to the east, and to the west, to the north, and to the south; and even now let him that goeth to the east, teach them that shall be converted to flee to the west; and this is the consequence of that which is to come on the earth, and of secret combinations. Behold, thou shalt observe all these things, and great shall be thy reward. Thou shalt observe to keep the mysteries of the kingdom unto thyself, for it is not given to the world to know the mysteries. The laws which ye have received, and shall hereafter receive, shall be sufficient for you both here, and in the New Jerusalem. Therefore, he that lacketh knowledge, let him ask of me and I will give him liberally, and upbraid him not. Lift up your hearts and rejoice, for unto you the kingdom has been given; even so. Amen.

The priests and teachers, shall have their stewardship given them even as the members; and the elders are to assist the bishop in all things, and he is to see that their families are supported out of the property which is consecrated to the Lord, either a stewardship, or otherwise, as may be thought best by the elders & bishop.

Behold, verily I say unto you, that whatever persons among you having put away their companions for the cause of fornication, or in other words, if they shall testify before you in all lowliness of heart that this is the case, ye shall not cast them out from among you; but if ye shall find that any persons have left their companions for the sake of adultery, and they themselves are of the offenders, and their companions are living, they shall be cast out from among you. And again I say unto you, that ye shall be watchful and careful, with all inquiry, that ye receive none such among you if they are married, and if they are not married, they shall repent of all their sins, or ye shall not receive them.

COMMANDMENT FOR KEEPING THE SABBATH, &c.

BEHOLD, saith the Lord, blessed are they who have come up unto this land with an eye single to my glory, according to my commandments; for them that live shall inherit the earth, and them that die shall rest from all their labours [labors], and their works shall follow them, and they shall receive a crown in the mansions of my father, which I have prepared for them; yea, blessed are they whose feet stand upon the land of Zion, who have obeyed my gospel, for they shall receive for their reward the good things of the earth, and it shall bring forth in its strength; and they also, shall be crowned with blessings from above; yea and with commandments not a few; and with revelations in their time, they that are faithful and diligent before me. Wherefore I give unto them a commandment saying thus: thou shalt love the Lord thy God with all thy heart, with all thy might, mind, and strength; and in the name of Jesus Christ thou shalt serve him. Thou shalt love thy neighbour [neighbor] as thyself. Thou shalt not steal. Neither commit adultery, nor kill, nor do any thing like unto it. Thou shalt thank the Lord thy God in all things. Thou shalt offer a sacrifice unto the Lord thy God in righteousness, even that of a broken heart and a contrite spirit; and that thou mayest more fully keep thy self unspoted [unspotted] from the world, thou shalt go to the house of prayer and offer up thy sacraments upon my holy day, for verily this is a day appointed unto you to rest from your labours [labors], and to pay thy devotions unto the most high: nevertheless thy vows shall be offered up in righteousness on all days, and at all times, but remember that on this, the Lord's day, thou shalt offer thine oblations, and thy sacraments, unto the most high, confessing thy sins unto thy brethren, and before the Lord; and on this day thou shalt do none other thing, only let thy food be prepared with singleness of heart, that thy fasting may be perfect, or in other words, that thy joy may be full. Verily this is fasting and prayer; or, in other words, rejoicing and prayer. And in as much as ye do these things with thanksgiving, with cheerful hearts, and countenances, (not with much laughter, for this is sin,) but with a glad heart, and a cheerful countenance: verily I say, that in as much as ye do this the fulness [fullness] of the earth is yours; the beasts of the fields, and the fowls of the air, and that which climbeth upon the trees, and walketh upon the earth, yea, and the herb, and the good things which cometh of the earth, whether for food or for raiment, or for houses, or for barns, or for orchards, or for gardens, or for vineyards; yea, all things which cometh of the earth, in the season thereof, is made for the benefit and the use of man, both to please the eye, and to gladden the heart; yea, for food and for raiment, for taste, and for smell, to strengthen the body, and to enliven the soul; and it pleaseth God that he hath given all these things unto men; for unto this end were they made, to be used with judgment, not to excess, neither by extortion; and in nothing doth man offend God or against none is his wrath kindled, save those who confess not his hand in all things and obey not his commandments. Behold this is according to the law and the prophets. Wherefore trouble me no more concerning this matter, but learn that he that doeth the works of righteousness, shall receive his reward, even peace in this world, and eternal life in the world to come. I the Lord have spoken it and the spirit beareth record. Amen.

A VISION.

HEAR, O ye Heavens, and give ear, O earth, and rejoice ye inhabitants thereof, for the Lord he is God, and beside him there is none else; and great is his wisdom; marvelous are his ways; and the extent of his doings, none can find out; his purposes fail not, neither are there any who can stay his hand: from eternity to eternity, he is the same, and his years never fail.

I the Lord am merciful and gracious unto them who fear me, and delight to honor them who serve me in righteousness, and in truth; great shall be their reward, and eternal shall be their glory; and unto them will I reveal all mysteries; yea, all the hidden mysteries of my Kingdom from days of old; and for ages to come will I make known unto them the good pleasure of my will concerning all things; yea, even the wonders of eternity shall they know, and things to come will I show them, even the things of many generations; their wisdom shall be great, and their understanding reach to Heaven; before them the wisdom of the wise shall perish, and the understanding of the prudent shall come to nought [naught]; for by my Spirit will I enlighten them, and by my power will I make known unto them the secrets of my will; yea, even those things which eye has not seen, nor ear heard, nor yet entered into the heart of man.

We, Joseph and Sidney, being in the Spirit on the sixteenth of February, in the year of our Lord, one thousand eight hundred and thirty two, and through the power of the Spirit, our eyes were opened, and our understandings were enlightened, so as to see and understand the things of God; even things which were from the biginning [beginning] before the world was, which was ordained of the Father, through his only begotten Son, who was in the bosom of the Father, even from the beginning, of whom we bear record, and the record which we bear is the fulness [fullness] of the Gospel of Jesus Christ, which is in the Son whom we saw and with whom we conversed in the Heavenly Vision; for as we sat doing the work of translation, which the Lord had appointed unto us, we came to the twenty ninth verse of the fifth chapter of John, which was given unto us thus: speaking of the resurrection of the dead who should hear the voice of the Son of man, and shall come forth; they who have done good in the resurrection of the just, and they who have done evil in the resurrection of the unjust. Now this caused us to marvel, for it was given us of the Spirit; and while we meditated upon these things, the Lord touched the eyes of our understandings, and they were opened, and the glory of the Lord shone round about; and we beheld the glory of the Son, on the right hand of the Father, and received of his fulness [fullness]; and saw the holy angels, and they who are sanctified before his throne, worshiping [worshipping] God and the Lamb forever and ever. And now after the many testimonies which have been given of him, this is the testimony, last of all, which we give of him, that he lives; for we saw him, even on the right hand of God; and we heard the voice bearing record that he is the only begotten of the Father; that by him, and through him, and of him, the worlds are made, and were created; and the inhabitants thereof are begotten sons and daughters unto God. This we saw also and bear record, that an angel of God, who was in authority in the presence of God, who rebelled against the only begotten Son, (whom the Father loved, and who was in the bosom of the Father,) and was thrust down from the presence of God and the Son, and was called Perdition; for the Heavens wept over him; for he was Lucifer, even the son of the morning; and we beheld and lo, he is fallen! is fallen! even the son of the morning. And while we were yet in the Spirit, the Lord commanded us that we should write the Vision; for behold satan, that old serpent, even the devil, who rebelled against God, and sought to take kingdoms of our God, and of his Christ; wherefore he maketh war with the saints of God, and encompasses them about: And we saw a vision of the eternal sufferings of those wtth [with] whom he maketh war and overcometh, for thus came the voice of the Lord unto us.

Thus saith the Lord, concerning all those who know my power, and who have been made partakers thereof, and suffered themselves, through the power of the devil, to be overcome unto the denying of the truth, and the defying of my power: they are they who are the sons of perdition, of whom I say it had been better for them never to have been born; for they are vessels of wrath doomed to suffer the wrath of God, with the devil and his angels, throughout eternity: concerning whom I have said there is no forgiveness for them in this world nor in the world to come; having denied the Holy Ghost after having received it, and having denied the only begotten Son of the Father, crucifying him unto themselves, and putting him to an open shame: these are they who shall go away into the lake of fire and brimstone, with the devil and his angels, and the only ones on whom the second death shall have any power; yea, verily the only ones who shall not be redeemed in the due time of the Lord, after the sufferings of his wrath, who shall be brought forth by the resurrection of the dead, through the triumph & the glory of the Lamb; who was slain, who was in the bosom of the Father before the worlds were made. And this is the Gospel, the glad tidings which the voice out of the heavens bore record unto us, that he came into the world, even Jesus to be crucified for the world, and to bear the sins of the world, and to sanctify the world, and to cleanse it from all unrighteousness; that through him all might be saved, whom the Father had put into his power; and made by him who glorifieth the Father; and saveth all the world of his hands, except those sons of perdition, who denieth the Son after the Father hath revealed him: wherefore he saveth all save them, and these shall go away into everlasting punishment, which is endless punishment, which is eternal punishment, to reign with the devil and his angels throughout eternity, where their worm dieth not and the fire is not quenched, which is their torment, but the end thereof, neither the place thereof, and their torment, no man knoweth, neither was revealed, neither is, neither will be revealed unto man, save to them who are made partakers thereof: nevertheless I the Lord showeth it by vision unto many, but straightway shutteth it up again: wherefore the end, the width, the height, the depth, and the misery thereof, he understandeth not, neither any man save them who are ordained unto this condemnation. And we heard the voice saying, Write the Vision for lo, this is the end of the vision of the eternal sufferings of the ungodly!

And again, we bear record for we saw and heard, and this is the testimony of the Gospel of Christ, concerning them who come forth in the resurrection of the just: they are they who received the testimony of Jesus, and believed on his name, and were baptized after the manner of his burial, being buried in the water in his name, and this according to the commandment which he hath given, that, by keeping the commandment, they might be washed and cleansed from all their sins, and receive the Holy Ghost by the laying on of the hands of him who is ordained and sealed unto this power; and who overcome by faith, and are sealed by that Holy Spirit of promise, which the Father shedeth forth upon all those who are just and true: they are they who are the church of the first born: they are they into whose hands the Father hath given all things: they are they who are priests and kings, who having received of his fulness [fullness], and of his glory, are priests of the most High after the order of Melchisedek [Melchisedec] which was after the order of Enoch, which was after the order of the only begotten Son: wherefore, as it is written, they are gods, even the sons of God: wherefore all things are theirs, whether life or death, or things present, or things to come, all are theirs, and they are Christ's, and Christ is God's; and they shall overcome all things: wherefore let no man glory in man, but rather let him glory in God, who shall subdue all enemies under his feet: these shall dwell in the presence of God and his Christ forever and ever: these are they whom he shall bring with him, when he shall come in the clouds of heaven, to reign on the earth over his people: these are they who shall have part in the first resurrection: these are they who shall come forth in the resurrection of the just: these are they who are come unto mount Zion, and unto the city of the living God, the heavenly place, the holiest of all: these are they who have come to an innumerable company of angels; to the general assembly and church of Enoch, and of the first born: these are they whose names are written in Heaven, where God and Christ is the judge of all: these are they who are just men made perfect through Jesus the Mediator of the new covenant, who wrought out this perfect atonement through the shedding of his own blood: these are they whose bodies are celestial, whose glory is that of the Son, even of God the highest of all; which glory the Sun of the firmament is written of as being typical.

And again, we saw the Terrestrial world, and behold and lo! these are they who are of the terrestrial, whose glory differeth from that of the church of the first born, who have received of the fulness [fullness] of the Father, even as that of the Moon differeth from the Sun of the firmament. Behold, these are they who died without law; and also they who are the spirits of men kept in prison, whom the Son visited and preached the Gospel unto them, that they might be judged according to men in the flesh, who received not the testimony of Jesus in the flesh, but afterwards received it: these are they who are honorable men of the earth, who were blinded by the craftiness of men: these are they who receive of his glory, but not of his fulness [fullness]: these are they who receive of the presence of the Son, but not of the fulness [fullness] of the Father: wherefore they are bodies terrestrial, and not bodies celestial, and differeth in glory as the Moon differeth from the Sun: these are they who are not valiant in the testimony of Jesus: wherefore they obtained not the crown over the kingdoms of our God. And now this is the end of the vision which we saw of the terrestrial, that the Lord commanded us to write while we were yet in the Spirit.

And again, we saw the glory of the Telestial, which glory is that of the lesser, even as the glory of the stars differeth from that of the glory of the Moon in the firmament: these are they who receive not the Gospel of Christ, neither the testimony of Jesus: these are they who deny not the Holy Ghost: these are they who are thrust down to hell: these are they who shall not be redeemed from the devil, until the last resurrection, until the Lord, even Christ the Lamb, shall have finished his work: these are they who receive not of his fulness [fullness] in that eternal world, but of the Holy Ghost through the administration of the terrestrial; and the terrestrial through the administration of the celestial; and also the telestial receive it of the administering of angels, who are appointed to minister for them, or who are appointed to be ministering spirits for them, for they shall be heirs of salvation.-And thus we saw in the Heavenly vision, the glory of the telestial which surpasseth all understanding; and no man knoweth it except him to whom God hath revealed it. And thus we saw the glory of the terrestrial, which excelleth in all things the glory of the telestial, even in glory, and in power, and in might, and in dominion. And thus we saw the glory of the celestial, which excelleth in all things where God, even the Father, reigneth upon his throne forever and ever: before whose throne all things bow in humble reverence and giveth him glory forever and ever. They who dwell in his presence are the church of the first born; and they see as they are seen, and know as they are known, having received of his fulness [fullness] and of his grace; and he maketh them equal in power, and in might, and in dominion. And the glory of the celestial is one, even as the glory of the Sun is one. And the glory of the Terrestrial is one, even as the glory of the Moon is one. And the glory of the Telestial is one, even as the glory of the stars is one: for as one star differeth from another star in glory, even so differeth one from another in glory in the telestial world: for these are they who are of Paul, and of Apollos, and Cephas: they are they who say, there are some of one and some of another; some of Christ; and some of John; and some of Moses; and some of Elias; and some of Esaias; and some of Isaiah; and some of Enoch, but received not the Gospel; neither the testimony of Jesus; neither the prophets; neither the everlasting covenant; last of all: these are they who will not be gathered with the saints, to be caught up into the church of the first born, and received into the cloud: these are they who are liars, and sorcerers, and adulterers, and whoremungers [whoremongers], and whosoever loveth and maketh a lie: these are they who suffer the wrath of God on the earth: these are they who suffer the vengeance of eternal fire: these are they who are cast down to hell and suffer the wrath of Almighty God until the fulness [fullness] of times, when Christ shall have subdued all enemies under his feet, and shall have perfected his work, when he shall deliver up the kingdom and present it unto his Father spotless, saying: I have overcome and trodden the wine-press alone, even the wine-press of the fierceness of the wrath of Almighty God: then shall he be crowned with the crown of his glory, to sit on the throne of his power to reign forever and ever. But behold and lo, we saw the inhabitants of the telestial world, that they were in number as innumerable as the stars in the firmament of Heaven, or as the sand upon the sea shore, and heard the voice of the Lord saying: These all shall bow the knee, and every tongue shall confess to him who sitteth upon the throne forever and ever: for they shall be judged according to their works; and every man shall receive according to his own works, and his own dominion, in the mansions which are prepared; and they shall be servants of the most High, but where God and Christ dwells they cannot come, worlds without end. This is the end of the vision which we saw, which we were commanded to write while we were yet in the Spirit.

But great and marvelous are the works of the Lord and the mysteries of his kingdom which he showed unto us, which surpasseth all understanding in glory, and in might, and in dominion, which he commanded us we should not write, while we were yet in the Spirit, and are not lawful for man to utter; neither is man capable to make them known, for they are only to be seen and understood by the power of the Holy Ghost; which God bestows on those who love him and purify themselves before him; to whom he grants this privilege of seeing and knowing for themselves; that through the power and manifestation of the Spirit, while in the flesh, they may be able to bear his presence in the world of glory. And to God and the Lamb be glory, and honor, and dominion, forever and ever. Amen.

Selected.

THE EXCELLENCE OF SCRIPTURE.

THE incomparable excellency which is in the sacred Scriptures, will fully appear, if we consider the matters contained in them under this threefold capacity. 1. As matters of divine revelation. 2. As a rule of life. 3. As containing that covenant of grace which relates to man's eternal happiness.

1. Consider the Scripture generally, as containing in it matters of divine revelation, and therein the excellency of the Scripture appears in two things. 1. The matters which are revealed. 2. The manner in which it is revealed.

1. The matter which are revealed in Scripture, may be considered these three ways. 1. As they are matters of the greatest weight and moment. 2. As matters of the greatest depth and mysteriousness. 3. As matters of the most universal satisfaction of the minds of men.

1. They are matters of the greatest moment and importance for men to know. The wisdom of men is most known by the weight of the things they speak; and therefore that wherein the wisdom of God is discovered, cannot contain any thing that is mean and trivial; they must be matters of the highest importance, which the Supreme Ruler of the world vouchsafes to speak to men concerning: and such we shall find the matters which God hath revealed in his word to be, which either concern the rectifying our apprehensions of his nature, or making known to men their state and condition, or discovering the way whereby to avoid eternal misery. Now which is there of these three, which, supposing God to discover his mind to the world, it doth not highly become him to speak to men of?

1. What is there which doeth more highly concern men to know, than God himself? or what more glorious and excellent object could he discover than himself to the world? There is nothing certainly which should more commend the Scripture to us, than that thereby we may grow more acquainted with God, that we may know more of his nature, and all his perfections, and many of the great reasons of his actings in the world. We may by them understand with safety what the eternal purposes of God were as to the way of man's recovery by the death of his son; we may there see and understand the great wisdom of God; not only in the contrivance of the world,

and ordering of it, but in the gradual revelations of himself to his people, by what steps he trained up his church till the fulness [fullness] of time was come; what his aim was in laying such a load of ceremonies on his people the Jews; by what steps and degrees he made way for the full revelation of his will to the world by speaking in these last days by his son, after he had spoken at sundry times and divers manners by the prophets, &c. unto the fathers. In the Scriptures we read the most rich and admirable discoveries of divine goodness, and all the ways and methods he useth in alluring sinners to himself; with what majesty he commands, with what importunity he woos men's souls to be reconciled to him; with what f-vor [favor] he embraceth, with what tenderness he chastiseth, with what bowels he pitieth those who have chosen him to be their God! With what power he supporteth, with what wisdom he directeth, with what cordials he refresheth the souls of such who are dejected under the sense of his displeasure, and yet their love is sincere towards him! With what profound humility, what holy boldness, what becoming distance, and yet what restless importunity do we therein find the souls of God's people addressing themselves to him in prayer! With what cheerfulness do they serve him, with what confidence do they trust him, with what resolutions do they adhere to him in all straits and difficulties, with what patience do they submit to his will in their greatest extremities! How fearful are they of sinning against God, how careful to please him, how regardless of suffering, when they must choose either that or sinning, how little apprehensive of men's displeasure, while they enjoy the favor of God! Now all these things which are so fully and pathetically expressed in Scripture, do abundantly set forth to us the exuberancy and pleonasm of God's grace and goodness towards his people, which makes them delight so much in him, and be so sensible of his displeasure. But above all other discoveries of God's goodness, his sending his son into the world to die for sinners, is that which the Scripture sets forth with the greatest life and eloquence. By eloquence, I mean not an artificial composure of words, but the gravity, weight, and persuasiveness of the matter contained in them. And what can tend more to melt our frozen hearts into a current of thankful obedience to God than the vigorous reflection of the beams of God's love through Jesus Christ upon us? Was there ever so great an expression of love heard of? nay, was it possible to be imagioned [imagined], that God who perfectly hates sin, should himself offer the pardon of it, and send his son into the world to secure it to the sinner, who doth so heartily repent of his sins, as to deny himself and take up his cross and follow Christ! Well might the Apostle say, "This is a faithful saying, and worthy of all acceptation, that Jesus Christ came into the world to save sinners." How dry and sapless are all the voluminous discourses of philosophers, compared with this sentence! How jejune and unsatisfactory are all the discoveries they had of God and his goodness, in comparison of what we have by the Gospel of Christ! Well might Paul then say, "That he determined to know nothing but Christ and him crucified." Christ crucified is the library which triumphant souls will be studying to all eternity. This is the only library which to commend is the true IATREION PSUCHES, [Greek.] that which cures the soul of all its maladies and distempers; other knowledge makes men's minds giddy and flatulent, this settles and composes them; other knowledge is apt to swell men into high conceits and opinions of themselves, this brings them to the truest view of themselves, and thereby to humility and sobriety; other knowledge leaves men's hearts as it found them, this alters them and makes them better. So transcendent an excellency is there in the knowledge of Christ crucified above the sublimest speculations in the world!

And is not this an inestimable benefit we enjoy by the Scripture, that therein we can read and converse with all these expressions of God's love and goodness, and that in his own language? Shall we admire and praise what we meet with in Heathen philosophers, which is generous and handsome; and shall we not adore the infinite fulness [fullness] of the Seriptures [Scriptures], which run over with continued expressions of that and a higher nature? What folly is it to magnify those lean kine, the notions of philosophers, and to contemn that fat, the plenty and fulness [fullness] of the Scriptures?- If there be not more valuable and excellent discoveries of the divine nature and perfections, if there be not far more excellent directions and rules of practice in the Sacred Scriptures, than in the sublimest of all the philosiphers [philosophers], then let us leave our full ears, and feed upon the thin. But certainly no sober and rational spirit, that puts any value upon the knowledge of God, but on the same account that he doth prize the discourses of any philosophers concerning God, he cannot but set a value of a far higher nature on the word of God. And as the goodness of God is thus discovered in Scripture, so is his justice and holiness: we have therein recorded the most remarkable judgments of God upon contumacious sinners, the severest denunciations of a judgment to come against all that live in sin, the exactest precepts of holiness in the world; and what can be desired more to discover the holiness of god, than we find in Scripture concerning him? If therefore acquaintance with the nature, perfection, designs of so excellent a being as God is, be a thing desirable to human nature, we have the greatest cause to admire the excellency and adore the fulness [fullness] of the Scriptures, which gives us so large, rational, and complete account of the being and attributes of God. And which tends yet more to commend the Scriptures to us, those things which the Scripture doth most fully discover concerning God, do not at all contradict those prime and common notions which are in our natures concerning him, but do exceedingly advance and improve them, and tend the most to regulate our conceptions and apprehensions of God, that we may not miscarry therein, as otherwise men are apt to do. For it being natural to men so far to love themselves, as to set the greatest value upon those excellencies which they think themselves most master of: thence men come to be exceedingly mistaken in their apprehensions of a deity, some attributing one thing as a perfection, another a different thing, according to their humours [humors] and inclinations. Thus imperious self-willed men are apt to cry up God's absolute power and dominion as his greatest perfection; easy and soft spirited men his patience and goodness; severe and rigid men his justice and severity: every one according to his humour [humor] and temper, making his god of his own complexion: and not only so, but in things remote enough from being perfections at all, yet because they are such things as they prize and value, they suppose of necessity they must be in God, as is evident in the Epicureans' ATARAXIA, [Greek.] by which they exclude providence, as hath already been observed. And withal considering how very difficult it is for one who really believes that God is of a pure, just, and holy nature, and that he hath grievously offended him by his sins, to believe that this God will pardon him upon true repentance: it is thence necessary that God should make known himself to the world, to prevent our misconceptions of his nature, and to assure a suspicious, because guilty creature, how ready he is to pardon iniquity, tranigression [transgression], and sin, to such as unfeignedly repent of their follies, and return unto himself. Though the light of nature may dictate much to us of the benignity and goodness of the divine nature, yet it is hard to conceive that that should discover farther than God's general goodness to such as please him: but no foundation can be gathered thence of his readiness as to pardon offenders, which being an act of grace, must alone be discovered by his will. I cannot think the sun, moon, and stars are such itinerant preachers, as to unfold unto us the whole counsel and will of God upon repentance. It is not every star in the firmament can do that which the star once did to the wise men, lead them unto Christ. The sun in the heavens is no Parelius to the sun of righteousness. The best astronomer will never find the day-star from on high in the rest of his number. What St. Austin said of Tully's works, is true of the whole volume of creation. There are admirable things to be found in them: but the name of Christ is not legible there. The world of redemption is not engraven on the works of providence; if it had, a particular divine revelation had been unnecessary, and the apostles were sent on a needless errand, which the world had understood without their preaching, viz. "That God was in Christ reconciling the world unto himself, not imputing to men their trespasses, and hath committed to them the ministry of reconciliation." How was the word of reconciliation committed to them if it were common to them with the whole frame of the world? and the apostle's query elsewhere might have been easily answered, How can men hear without a preacher? for then they might have known the way of salvation, without any special messenger sent to deliver it to them. I grant that God's long suffering and patience is intended to lead men to repetence [repentance], and that some general collections might be made from providence of the placability of God's nature, and that God never left himself without a witness of his goodness in the world, being kind to the unthankful, and doing good, in giving rain and fruitful seasons. But though these things might sufficiently discover to such who were apprehensive of the guilt of sin, that God did not act according to his greatest severity, and thereby did give men incouragement [encouragement] to hearken out and inquire after the true way of being reconciled to God; yet all this amounts not to a firm foundation for faith as to the remission of sin, which doth support God himself publishing an act of grace and indemnity to the world, wherein he assures the pardon of sin to such as truly repent and unfeignedly beleive [believe] his holy Gospel. Now is not this an inestimable advantage we enjoy by the Scriptures, that therein we understand what God himself hath discovered of his own nature and perfections, and of his readiness to pardon sin upon those gracious terms of faith and repentance, and that which necessarily follows from these two, hearty and sincere obedience?

2. The Scriptures give the most faithful representation of the state and condition of the soul of man. The world was almost lost in disputes concerning the nature, condition, and immortality of the soul before divine revelation was made known to mankind by the gospel of Christ; but "life and immortality was brought to light by the gospel," and the future state of the soul of man, not discovered in an uncertain Platonical way with the greatest light and evidence from that God who hath the supreme disposal of souls, and therefore best knows and understands them. The Scriptures plainly and fully reveal a judgment to come, in which God will judge the secrets of all hearts, when every one must give an account of himself unto God, and God will call men to give an account of their stewardship here, of all the receipts they have had from him, and the expenses they have been at, and the improvements they have made of the talents he put into their hands. So that the gospel of Christ is the fullest instrument of the discovery of the certainty of the future state of the soul, and the conditions which abide it, upon its being dislodged from the body. But this is not all which the Scripture discovers as to the sate of the soul; for it is not only a prospective

glass, reaching to its future state, but it is the most faithful looking-glass, to discover all the spots and deformities of the soul: and not only shows where they are, but when they came, what their nature is, and whither they tend. The true original of all that disorder and discomposure which is in the soul of man, is only fully and satisfactorily given us in the Word of God.

The nature and working of this corruption in man had never been so clearly manifested, had not the law and will of God been discovered to the world; that is the glass whereby we see the secret workings of those bees in our hearts, the corruption of our natures; that sets forth the folly of our imaginations, the unruliness of our passions, the distempers of our wills, and the abundant deceitfulness of our hearts.

And it is hard for the most Elephantine sinner (one of the greatest magnitude) so to trouble these waters, as not therein to discover the greatness of his own deformities. But that which tends most to awaken the drowsy, senseless spirits of men, the Scripture doth most fully describe the tendency of corruption, "that the wages of sin is death," and the issue of continuance in sin will be the everlasting misery of the soul, in a perpetual separation from the presence of God, and undergoing the lashes and severities of concience [conscience] to all eternity. What a great discovery is this of the faithfulness of God to the world, that he suffers not men to undo themselves without letting them know of it before hand, that they may avoid it! God seeks not to entrap men's souls, nor doth he rejoice in the misery and ruin of his creatures, but fully declares to them what the consequence and issue of their sinful practices will be, assures them of a judgment to come, declares his own future severity against contumacious sinners, that they might not think themselves surprised, and that if they had known there had been so much danger in sin, they would never have been such fools as for the sake of it to run into eternal misery. Now God to prevent this, with the greatest plainness and faithfulness, hath showed men the nature and danger of all their sins, and asks them before hand what they will do in the end thereof; whether they are able to bear his wrath, and wrestle with everlasting burnings? if not, he bids them bethink themselves of what they have done already, and repent and amend their lives, lest iniquity prove their ruin, and destruction overtake them, and that without remedy. Now if men have cause to prize and value a faithful monitor, one that tenders their good, and would prevent their ruin, we have cause excedingly [exceedingly] to prize and value the Scriptures, which gives us the truest representation of the state and condition of our souls.

3. The scripture discovers to us the only way of pleasing God and enjoying his favour [favor]. That clearly reveals the way (which man might have sought for to all eternity without particular revelation) whereby sins may be pardoned, and whatever we do may be acceptable unto God. It shows us that the ground of our acceptance with God, is through Christ, whom he hath made "a propitiation for the sins of the world," and who alone is the true and living way, whereby we may "draw near to God with a true heart, in full assurance of faith, having our hearts sprinkled from an evil conscience." Through Christ we understand the terms on which God will show favour [favor] and grace to the world, and by him we have ground of a PARRESIA [Greek.] access with freedom and boldness unto God. On his account we may hope not only for grace to subdue our sins, resist temptations, conquer the devil and the world; but having "fought this good fight, and finished our course by patient continuance in well doing, we may justly look for glory, honor, and immortality," and that 'crown of righteousness which is laid up for those who wait in faith,' holiness, and humility, for the appearance of Christ from heaven. Now what things can there be of greater moment and importance for men to know, or God to reveal, than the nature of God and ourselves the state and condition of our souls, the only way to avoid eternal misery and enjoy everlasting bliss!

The Scriptures discover not only matters of importance, but of the greatest depth and mysteriousness. There are many wonderful things in the law of God, things we may admire, but are never able to comprehend. Such are the eternal purposes and decrees of God, the doctrine of the Trinity, the incarnation of the Son of God, and the manner of the operation of the Spirit of God upon the souls of men, which are all things of great weight and moment for us to understand and believe that they are, and yet may be unsearchable to our reason, as to the particular manner of them. [(->) To be continued.]

THE SIMPLICITY OF THE SACRED WRITERS.

I CANNOT forbear taking notice of one other mark of integrity which appears in all the composition of the sacred writers, and particularly the Evangelists; and that is, the simple, unaffected, unornamental, and unostentatious manner, in which they deliver truths so important and sublime, and facts so magnificent and wonderful, as are capable, one would think, of lighting up a flame of oratory, even in the dullest and coldest breast. They speak of an angel descending from heaven to foretel [foretell] the miraculous conception of Jesus; of another proclaiming his birth, attended by a multitude of the heavenly host praising God, "and saying, Glory to God in the highest, and on earth peace, good will towards men;" of his star appearing in the East; of angels ministering to him in the wilderness; of his glory in the mount; of a voice twice heard from heaven, saying, "This is my beloved Son;" of innumerable miracles performed by him, & by his disciples in his name; of his knowing the thoughts of men; of his foretelling future events; of prodigies accompanying his crucifixion and death; of an angel decending [descending] in terrors, opening his sepulchre [sepulcher], and frightening away the soldiers who were set to guard it; of his rising from the dead, ascending into the heaven, and pouring down, according to his promise, the various and miraculous gifts of the Holy Spirit upon his apostles and disciples. All these amazing incidents do these inspired historians relate nakedly and plainly without any of the colourings [colorings] and heightenings of rhetoric, or so much as a single note of admiration; without making any comment or remark upon them, or drawing from them any conclusion in honor either of their master or themselves, or to the advantage of the religion they preached in his name; but contenting themselves with relating the naked truth, whether it seems to make for them or against them; without either magnifying on the one hand, or palliating on the other, they leave their cause to the unbiassed [unbiased] judgment of mankind, seeking, like genuine apostles of the Lord of truth, to convince rather than to persuade; and therefore coming, as St. Paul speaks of his preaching, "not with excellency of speech, not with enticing words of man's wisdom, but with demonstration of the spirit, and of power, that," adds he, "your faith should not stand in the wisdom of men, but in the power of God." And let it be remembered that he, who speaks this, wanted not learning, art, or aloquence [eloquence], as is evident from his speeches recorded in the Acts of the Apostles, and from the testimony of that great critic Longinus, who, in reckoning up the Grecian orators, places among them Paul of Tarsus; and surely, had they been left solely to the suggestions and guidance of human wisdom, they would not have failed to lay hold on such topics, as the wonders of their master's life, and the transcendent purity and perfection of the noble, generous, benevolent morality contained in his precepts, furnished them with. These topics, I say, greater than ever Tully, or Demosthenes, or Plato, were possessed of, mere human wisdom would doubtless have prompted them to make use of, in order to recommend, in the strongest manner, the religion of Jesus Christ to mankind, by turning their attention to the divine part of his character, and hiding, as it were in a blaze of heavenly light and glory, his infirmities, his sufferings, and his death. Had they called to their assistance of the arts of composition, rhetoric, and logic, who would have blamed them for it? Not those persons, I presume, who, dazzled and captivated with the glittering ornaments of human wisdom, made a mock at the simplicity of the Gospel, and think it wit to ridicule the style and language of the Holy Scriptures. But the all-wise Spirit of God, by whom these sacred writers were guided into all truth, thought fit to direct or permit them to proceed in a different method; a method, however, very analogous to that in which he has been pleased to reveal himself to us in the great book of nature, the stupendous frame of the universe; all whose wonders he hath judged it sufficient to lay before us in silence, and expects from our observations the proper comments and deductions, which have endued us with reason, he hath enabled us to make. And tho' a careless and superficial spectator may fancy he perceives even in this fair volume many inconsistencies, defects, and superfluities; yet to a diligent, unprejudiced, and rational inquirer, who will take pains to examine the laws, consider and compare the several parts, and regard their use and tendency, with reference to the whole design of this amazing structure, as far as his short abilities can carry him, there will appear, in those instances which he is capable of knowing, such evidence characters of wisdom, goodness and power, as will leave him no room to doubt to their author, or to suspect that in those particulars which he has not examined, or to a thorough knowledge of which he cannot perhaps attain, there is nothing but folly, weakness, and malignity. The same thing might be said of the written book, the second volume, if I may so speak, of the revelations of God, the Holy Scriptures. For as in the first, so also in this are there many passages, that to a cursory, unobserving reader appear idle, unconnected, unaccountable, and inconsistent with those marks of truth, wisdom, justice, mercy, and benevolence, which in others are so visible, that the most careless and inattentive cannot but decern [discern] them. And even these, many of them, at least, will often be found, upon a closer and stricter examination, to accord and coincide with the other more plain and more intelligible passages, and to be no heterogeneous parts of one and the same wise and harmonious composition. In both, indeed, in the natural as well as the moral book of God, there are, and ever will be, many difficulties, which the wit of man may never be able to resolve; but will a wise philosopher, because he cannot comprehend every thing he sees, reject for that reason all the truths that lie within his reach, and let a few inexplicable difficulties over-balance the many plain and infallible evidences of the finger of God, which appear in all parts, both of his created and written works? Or will he presume so far upon his own wisdom, as to say, God ought to have expressed himself more clearly? The point and exact degree of clearness, which will equally suit the different capacities of men in different ages and countries, will I believe, be found more difficult to fix than is imagined; since what is clear to one man in a certain situation of mind, time, and place, will inevitably be obscure to another, who views it in other circumstances. How various and even contradictory are the readings and comments, which several men, in the several ages and climates of the world, have made upon nature! And yet her characters are equally legible, and her laws equally intelligible, in all times and in all places: "There is no speech nor language where her voice is not heard: her sound is gone out through all the earth, and her words to the end of the world." And these misrepresentations therefore, and misconstructions, of her works, are chargeable only upon mankind, who have set themselves to study them with various degrees of capacity, application, and impartiality. The question then should be, why hath God given men such various talents? And not, why hath not God expressed himself more clearly? And the answer to this question, as far as it concerns man to know, is, that God will require of him according to what he hath, and not according to what he hath not. If what is necessary for all to know, is knowable by all; those men upon whom God hath been pleased to bestow capacities and faculties superior to the vulgar, have certainly no just reason to complain of this having left them materials for the exercise of those talents, which, if all things were equally plain to all men, would be of no great advantage to the possesrors [possessors]. If therefore, there are in the sacred writings, as well as in the works of natnre [nature], many passages hard to be understood, it were to be wished, that the wise and learned, instead of being offended at them, and teaching others to be so too, would be persuaded that both God and man expect that they would set themselves to consider and examine them carefully and impartially, and with a sincere desire of discovering and embracing the truth, not with an arrogant unphilosophical conceit of their being already sufficiently wise and knowing. And then I doubt not but most of these objections to revelation, which are now urged with the greatest confidence, would be cleared up and removed, like those formerly made to Creation, and the Being and Providence of God, by those most ignorant, most absurd, and yet most self-sufficient pretenders to reason and philosophy, the Atheists and Sceptics [Skeptics].-[West.]

Aristotle considers friendship as of three kinds; one arising from virtue, another from pleasure, and another from interest; but justly determine, that there can be no true friendship, which is not founded in virtue.

A deaf and dumb pupil, when asked in writing, what is Eternity? wrote upon his slate with his pencil, THE LIFE TIME OF THE ALMIGHTY.

CONTENTS.

Of this (July) number of the Evening and the Morning Star.

THE EVENING AND THE MORNING STAR.

[COMMUNICATED.]

THE ELDERS IN THE LAND OF ZION TO THE CHURCH OF CHRIST SCATTERED ABROAD.

BRETHREN, We think it proper to give you some general information respecting the present state of the church in Zion, and also the work of the gathering. Notwithstanding that nearly all christendom doubt the propriety of receiving revelations for the government of the church of Christ in this age, and generally adopt the Scriptures of the old and new testament as the only rule of faith and practice, yet we believe, from the Scriptures of truth, that to every church in the past ages, which the Lord recognized to be his, he gave revelations wisely calculated to govern them in the peculiar situation and circumstances under which they were placed, and to enable them by authority to do the peculiar work which they were to perform. The Bible contains revelations given at different times to different people, under different circumstances, as will be seen by editorial articles in this paper. The old world was destroyed for rejecting the revelations of God, given to them through Noah. The Israelites were destroyed in the wilderness for dispising [despising] the revelations given to them through Moses; and Christ said that the world, in the days of the apostles, should be condemned for not receiving the word of God through them: thus we see that the judgments of God in the past ages have come upon the people, not so much for neglecting the revelations given to their forefathers, as for rejecting those given immediately to themselves. Of the blessings of heaven it may be said, they have always rested upon the heads of those to whom they were promised: Therefore, seeing that it not only was, but as long as God remains the same, always will be the privelige [privilege] of the true church to receive revelations, containing blessings and cursings, peculiarly adapted to itself as a church. We conclude it is a mistaken notion that the Scriptures of the old and new testament are the only rule of faith and practice; nevertheless, inasmuch as the precepts and examples contained in them are truly applicable to us, under our particular circumstances, we are bound to be governed by them; and we also can receive much benefit from such prophecies as point out the events that shall take place in our day and age: of these there are many, both in the old and new testament. They speak plainly of great things that shall be accomplished in the last days; such as preaching of the everlasting gospel to all nations; the gathering of the elect from the four winds of heaven; the building up of Zion and Jerusalem, or the ingathering of the remnants of Jacob, and the planting them in the lands of their fathers' inheritance: the necessary preparation to meet the Savior at his second coming, with all his saints to dwell with them in the millennium reign. And now, who with the Bible in his hand, can suppose that these great and marvelous works can be accomplished by the church without more revelations from the Lord? We cannot, for we worship the God of Israel, in whom there is neither variableness nor shadow of turning; consequently as in days of old, so in these last days, he has given us revelations by which we may know how to organize the church of Christ, and by his authority to perform the work which he has enjoined upon us. And now brethren, if we wish for blessings upon this church, we must walk humble before the Lord, and observe to keep all his commandments. Notwithstanding the work of the gathering will be accomplished, we believe, in a speedy manner, yet the Lord has commanded that it shall not be done in haste, nor by flight, but that all things shall be prepared before you; and for this purpose he has made it the duty of the Bishop or Agent in the land of Zion, to make known, from time to time, the privileges of the land, to the conferences, which may determine and make known how many can be accommodated. And the saints will remember that the Bishop in the land of Zion, will not receive say, as wise stewards, without they bring a recommend from the Bishop in Ohio, or from three elders. The elders therefore, will be careful not to recommend and send up churches to this place, without first receiving information from the bishop in Ohio, or in the land of Zion, that they can be accommodated when they arrive, so as to be settled without confusion, which would produce pestilence. Therefore, if a church is desirous to come to the land of Zion, we would recommend, that first, by letter or otherwise, they make known their desires and their situation to the Bishop in Ohio, or in the land of Zion, and receive information from them before they start. Brethren will perceive as well as we, that where churches of fifty or a hundred souls each, are coming to the land of Zion from different parts of the nation, and, as soon will be the case, from different nations, without a knowledge of each other, they would, when they arrive, be in a state of confusion, and labor under many disadvantages, which might be avoided by strictly observing the rules and regulations of the church. Moreover by being in haste, and forcing the sale of property, unreasonable sacrifices have been made, and although this is a day of sacrifice and tithing, yet to make lavish and unreasonable sacrifices, is not well pleasing in the sight of the Lord.

It is about one year since the work of the gathering commenced, in which time between three & four hundred have arrived here and are mostly located upon their inheritances, and are generally in good health and spirits and are doing well. The expenses of journeying and settling here, together with the establishing of a printing office and store, have probably exceeded the expectations of our brethren abroad, and although Zion, according to the prophets, is to become like Eden or the garden of the Lord, yet, at present it is as it were but a wilderness and desert, and the disadvantages of settling in a new country, you know, are many and great: Therefore, prudence would dictate at present the churches abroad, come not up to Zion, until preparations can be made for them, and they receive information as above. The prospect for crops, in this region of country, is, at present, tolerable good, but calls for provisions will undoubtedly be considerable, for besides the emigration of the whites, the government of the United States is settling the Indians, (or remnants of Joseph) immediately to the west, and they must be fed.

Brethren, we drop the above remarks for your benefit, until you can have the revelation to peruse for yourselves, which will be published as soon as they can be consistently. Although the Lord has said, that it is his business to provide for his saints in these last days, yet, remember he is not bound so to do, unless we observe his sayings and keep them.

***Our Elders abroad, may do much good by obtaining subscribers for the Star, and transmit the money by mail, to us, or the Bishop in Ohio.

HOSEA CHAPTER III.

WE select this chapter for a few comments, because it contains some figures of speech, as well as plain prophecy.

Then said the Lord unto me, Go yet, love a woman beloved of her friend, yet an adulteress, according to the love of the Lord toward the children of Israel, who look to other Gods, and love flagons of wine. So I bought her to me for fifteen pieces of silver, and for a homer of barley, and a half homer of barley: and I said unto her, Thou shalt abide for me many days; thou shalt not play the harlot, and thou shalt not be for an other man: so will I also be for thee. For the children of Israel shall abide many days without a king, and without a prince, and without a sacrifice, and without an image, and without an ephod, and without a teraphim: Afterwards shall the children of Israel return, and seek the Lord their God, and David their king; and shall fear the Lord and his goodness in the latter days.

(->) Notwithstanding some, or nearly all professing denominations of what are called Christians, have invented a general rule to spiritualize the Scripture, yet these sacred records carry, on almost every page, a very different idea: For instance, when God said, let there be light and there was light, every rational man, that believes the word of God, must know it was temporally so, because the light continues yet. When God told Noah to prepare an Ark, for Behold I even I do bring a flood of waters upon the earth to destroy all flesh, who dare say it was not literally fulfilled? When Moses led the children of Israel out of Egypt, and Pharaoh followed after and was swallowed up in the Red Sea, what spiritual construction will turn this mighty scene, from the power of God naturally displayed to man? When the Lord told Ahaz, Behold a virgin shall conceive and bear a son, and Jesus Christ came in the flesh: not only them that saw him and believed then, but those who have believed and have been baptized, and have received the gift of the Holy Ghost since, know that this prophecy was literally fulfilled as foretold. Using such literal examples far a guide, we shall commence literalizing this Chapter of Hosea, and say the first verse alluded to sending the gospel to the Gentiles, which Peter and Paul afterwards fulfilled.-No one can dispute that the woman means the church, for the Lord has created a new thing in the earth: A woman shall compass a man, and the church of Christ will eventually triumph over the man of sin, and Satan will be bound. The second and third verses may refer to the son of perdition, who sold his master for money.-Then salvation to the Gentiles: which salvation was to continue many days, viz: to the present day. The fourth verse shows the time that the children of Israel were to remain scattered abroad, without the sacred things which God gave unto them when they were to remain scattered abroad, without the sacred things which God gave unto them when they were in favour [favor] with him. They were even to do without the Teraphim, [Urim & Thummim, perhaps] or sacred spectacles or declarers; supposed to be the same called gods and images when Jacob fled, from Laban. For Jacob was a man of God and did not worship idols or images. The original in Hebrew is Teraphim. Moses when blessing the tribes in the 33rd of Deuteronomy, says: Let thy Thummim and thy Urim be with thy Holy one. This brings to mind that important information on the same subject, which is recorded in the second Chapter of II Maccabees, which the wisdom of man has seen fit to call Apocrypha. It reads thus:

It is also found in the records, that Jeremy the prophet commanded them that were carried away to take of the fire, as it has been signified: And how that the prophet, having given them the law, charged them not to forget the commandments of the Lord, and that they should not err in their minds, when they see images of silver and gold, with their ornaments. And with other such speeches exhorted he them, that the law should not depart from their hearts. It was also contained in the same writing, that the prophet, being warned of God, commanded the tabernacle and the ark to go with him, as he went forth into the mountain, where Moses climbed up, and saw the heritage of God. And when Jeremy came thither, he found a hollow cave, wherein he laid the tabernacle, and the ark, and the altar of incense, and so stopped the door. And some of those that followed him came to mark the way, but could not find it. Which when Jeremy perceived, he blamed them, saying, As for the place, it shall be unknown until the time that God gather his people together, and receive them unto mercy. Then shall the Lord shew [show] these things, and the glory of the Lord shall appear, and the cloud also, as it was shewed [showed] unto Moses, and as when Solomon desired that the place might be honourably [honorably] sanctified.

The fifth verse directs to the time of the gathering, and positively promises their return, which our Savior referred to, when he declared that he would send his angels and gather his Elect.-Here let it be known once for all, that Israel, the twelve tribes of Jacob, are the Elect of God. Isa. 45th and 4th and Romans 11th 28th which says, as touching the election, they are beloved for the fathers' sakes. Again, it not only promises the return of Israel in the latter days, but it declares that they shall seek the Lord their God, and David their King. Seek David their King! Here remember that David had been dead many years, for Hosea prophesied about 175 years before the Babylonish Captivity: It opens the meaning of the latter part of the 37th Chapter of Ezekiel, which speaking of the gathering of Israel, says that they shall dwell in the land that I have given unto Jacob my servant, and they shall dwell therein, they and their children, and their children's children for ever, and my servant David shall be their prince for ever. David must have had his eye upon the same thing when he said in the 71st Psalm, Thou shalt quicken me again, and shalt bring me up again from the depth of the earth. No man will attempt to say that the children of Israel have lived in the land of Jacob, governed by David as King or Prince, since God by the mouths of Hosea and Ezekiel declared, that such should be the case, in the latter days! The secret of the matter is, that God, in his infinite wisdom prepared the children of promise, the heirs of the Celestial kingdom, to live twice in the flesh on the earth, once in a state of probation; and once in a state of approbation, and this is the reason why Job exclaimed: For I know my Redeemer liveth, and he shall stand at the latter day upon the earth: and though after my skin worms destroy this body, yet in my flesh shall I see God. And again this accounts for the Redeemed out of every kindred, and tongue, and people and nation, which John the Revelator saw [Rev. Chap. 5.] who were made Kings and Priests to God, and reigned on earth or as it is written [Rev. Chap. 20.] They lived and reigned with Christ a thousand years.

ITEMS FOR THE PUBLIC

IN connexion [connection] with the star, we publish a weekly paper, entitled "The Upper Missouri Advertiser," It will contain sketches of the news of the day, politics, advertisements, and whatever tends to promote the interests of the Great West.

(->) An extract from the Prophecy of Enoch in our next number.

(->) The "Vision," which appears on the second page, is the greatest news that was ever published to man. It shows the economy of God, in preparing mansions for men: Blessed be the name of the Lord.

(->) Notwithstanding the Month of May was wet and cold, the weather, for some time past, has been such, that the prospect of the farmer is fair, and we have hopes of good crops.

(->) The frontier Indian war continues. There have been several killed on both sides. The government of the United States has appropriated $300,000 for this purpose, and we may calculate, the war will be prosecuted vigorously as far as necessary.

(->) The Cholera Morbus commenced its deadly work at Quebec, Lower Canada about the first of June. It is said to be severer, than in Europe. The will of God must be done whether by pestilence, famine, or the sword.

TO THE ELDERS OF THE CHURCH OF CHRIST, WHO PREACH GOOD TIDINGS TO THE WORLD

BRETHREN, As stars of the ensign, which is now set up for the benefit of all nations, you are to enlighten the world; you are to prepare the way for the people to come up to Zion; you are to instruct men how to receive the fulness [fullness] of the gospel, and the everlasting covenants, even them that were from the beginning; you are to carry the ARK OF SAFETY before the wondering multitudes, without fear, entreating, and beseeching all men to be saved; you are to set an example of meekness and humility before saints and sinners, as did the Savior; and when reviled you are not to revile again; you are to reason with men as in days of old, to bear patiently and answer as the spirit of truth shall direct, allowing all credit for every item of good. You are to walk in the valley of humility and pray for the salvation of all; yes, you are to pray for your enemies; and warn in compassion, without threatening the wicked with judgments which are to be poured upon the world hereafter. You have no right to take the judgments, which fell upon the ungodly before the flood, and pour them upon the head of this generation; you have no authority to use the judgments which God sent upon Pharaoh in Egypt, to terrify the inhabitants of America, neither have you any direction, by commandment, to collect the calamities of six thousand years, and paint them upon the curtain of these last days, to scare mankind to repentance; no; you are to preach the gospel, which is the power of God unto salvation, even glad tidings of great joy unto all people.

Again, you are not to take the blessings of an individual, or of a church, from the days of Enoch to the days of the apostles, and place them upon an individual or a church, in these last days; but you are to teach all men that they shall be judged according to their works: For, if God is the same yesterday, to-day, and forever, his reward is always with him, and his revelations and blessings, and judgments, before the flood, were fitted for that people and that time; in the days of Abraham, for that man and that time; in the days of Moses, for that man and that time; in the days of David, for that man and that time; in the days of Paul, for that man and that time; and now, for this generation, and this time: You therefore, must reason from the Bible and the Book of Mormon, with great care and not pervert the meaning of God's sacred word. If our Heavenly Father saw fit to destroy Sodom and Gomorah for their wickedness, Nineveh for its abomination, and Jerusalem for a transgression of his commandments, what have their destructions to do with the salvation of the world now? The Lord says vengeance is mine, and I will repay. Teach all men to trust in God and not in man, and do works meet for repentance.-Again, teach all men that God is a God of the living and not of the dead. Finally, whatever you do, do it with an eye single to the glory of god. You are the light of the world in matters of pure religion, and many souls may be required at your hands. Let the idea not leave you that, not only the eyes of the world, but the eyes of the angels and of God are upon you.

FOREIGN NEWS.

IT is a day of strange appearances. Every thing indicates something more than meets the eye. Every nation is opening events, which astonish mankind: Even the heart of man begins to melt at the prospect before it. The unquenchable thirst for news; the continuity of emigration; the wars and rumors of wars, with many other signs of the distress of nations, from the old world, (as it is called across the Ocean) whispers so loud to the understanding, that he that runs may read the label on the Eastern sky: The end is nigh. France is filled with a spirit of rebellion, and when the Cholera was sweeping its thousands, mobs were collecting to slay their tens of thousands. While the hospitals were crowded with the sick, and the groans of the dying filled the air, the fashionable French were holding Cholera Balls and dancing at the judgments of the almighty. In England, where an anxious multitude have been waiting for Reformation in government for years, disappointment is distruction [destruction]. The house of Lords has rejected the Reform bill, and the proud hearted Englishman says-Reform or Revolution! No stop there: for the sound comes across the Atlantic. Reform or ruin! All the Kingdoms of the East seem to be preparing to act the part allotted to them, when the Lord rebukes the nations. As on a morning of some, great festival, the church bell, the cannon, the small arms, the music, and the cheers of the multitude, arouse all to what is going on, and thunders to man: Behold the day! so also earthquakes wars, and rumors of wars, the distress of nations, the constant tide of emigration to the West, the wide spreading ravages of the Cholera Morbus, and the joy of the Saints of God as they come out of Babylon, alarms the world, and whispers to every mortal, watch ye, for the time is at hand for the second coming of Jesus Christ, the Redeemer of Israel, with peace on earth and good will to man. Watch the signs of his coming, that ye be not deceived.

Worldly Matters

DAVID Ritter of New Haven, with twelve hands, manufactures, $10,000 worth of Razor straps a year. And again the said David with five hands, turns off about $3,000 worth of marble monuments, chimney pieces, &c.

At an election in Montreal, L. C. a dreadful riot took place, which resulted in the death of several men.

ROMANCE OF REAL LIFE.-On Friday April 26, 1832, D. Falton, one of the coroners of this county, was called to view the bodies of Elizabeth Bird and Abraham Vandyck, found drowned in Brown's pond, town of Clinton. They were tied together around the waist, and from previous declarations, no doubt remained but that they had deliberately made way with themselves. They were seen going to the Pond on Wednesday preceding, she quite intoxicated, and it was supposed he not much better. They had divested themselves of their upper garments which were carefully deposited near the Lake, together with a bottle containing the remains of a pint of rum which they had purchased that morning, perhaps not an hour before they took their fatal plunge. Both were habitually intemperate.-[Poughkeepsie paper.]

We learn from the Wyoming Republican, that three children were recently scalded to death in Luzerne county. The mother was engaged in boiling soap, when the pot fell from the crane, and the contents were dashed over two children playing on the floor before the fire; and the third, which was on her lap, she dropped into the boiling liquid in her frightful endeavors to rescue the other two.

EMIGRANTS.-On Sunday last, fourteen hundred and forty six emigrants arrived in this city from Europe, and yesterday, four hundred and twenty eight. The number which arrived at Quebec on the 26th, 27th, and 28th of May, was two thousand, four hundred and eighty eight.-[N. Y. Com.]

A church bell of glass has been cast in Sweden; its diameter is six feet, and its tone is said to be finer than that of any metal.

BOSTON, MAY 18

Yesterday forenoon Mr. George W. Coombs was at work in the well of Mr. William T. Spear, Prince Street, about 36 feet from the surface, and Mr. William Elm about 8 feet below him, both in the employ of Mr. Isaac Scott, laying lead pipe, and using a furnace with charcoal, for soldering. Coombs complained of faintness and Elm went up to assist him; but, in passing the furnace he was likewise taken faint, yet succeeded in reaching the top, and calling assistance. Before it arrived, however, Mr. C. had fallen to the bottom. He was drawn up, and two physicians attended immediately; but life was extinct. Mr. C. was about 25 years of age, and has left a wife and child. It was the opinion of the physicians that the fumes of the charcoal caused his death.-[Daily Adv.]

BOSTON, MAY 18.

A young girl aged about nine years, daughter of Mr. Ezra Palmer, residing at No. 92, Ann street, whilst reaching out of a chamber window in the third story to arange [arrange] a bird cage, lost her balance and fell to the ground. In her fall, she struck on the shoulder of a young man who was passing at the moment, and thus, happily, her life was preserved. She has, however, suffered severely from contusions, broken bones, and dislocations.-[Transcript.]

In Augusta, on Wednesday, a squall took place, which blew out the gable end of a brick bilding [building] near the market, belonging to Mr. Bennock, which, falling on a small adjoining wood house killed two negroes that were in it, a woman, and child of three or four years old, and crippled two others. The wall was only one brick thick.-[Sa. Ga.]

GREAT FRESHET.-In consequence of a heavy rain which commenced on the 19th of May and continued till the 22d, the waters of the Kennebec river in Maine, rose to an unparalleled height. In many places it was 20 feet above low water mark, and has done immense damage, carrying away bridges, mills, houses and large quantities of lumber.

A gentleman, who within the past six months has visited nearly every principal town in the Valley of the Mississippi, has furnished the editor of the Journal of Commerce with a list, by which it appears that twenty four steamboats have been destroyed on the western waters, since the breaking up of the ice last spring.

PHENOMENON.-From the Poughkeepsie Telegraph, we learn that a piece of land, embracing an area of an acre and a half, on the eastern shore, in Dutchess county, three miles above Newburg, has sunk one hundred feet, so that the tops of the highest trees growing upon it, are scarcely level with the surrounding surface. It is supposed that a stream of water, flowing beneath the river, has finally washed away such a quantity of the supporting earth as to render this occurrence inevitable; if this be not a philosophical explanation, we must place the phenomenon to the credit of the theory of Capt. Symmes.-[N. Y. paper.]

THE COMET OF 1832.

On or about the 22d of next August Biela's Comet may be seen by means of telescopes somewhere near the direction of the seven stars. On the 19th of September, it will be visible to the naked eye just above the horizon in the North East, about 9 o'clock in the evening. About 10 o'clock in the evening of November 13th it will rise E. N. E., and will about that time appear the brightest. From the middle of October to the middle of November, it may be seen with great distinctness. August 22d its distance from the Earth will be 117,373,096 miles, and 157,479,530 from the Sun.-Its nearest approach to our planet will be on the 23d of October, when its distance from us will be 51,035,913 miles, and from the Sun 98,650,424. It will cross the Earth's orbit about the last of October, when it will be several hundred thousand miles farther from us than it will be when it passes its perihelion. Its nearest approach to the Sun will take place on the 28th of November when its distance from that planet will be 83,444,193 miles, and from us 67,952,845.-[N. E. Review.]

THE POLES.-The heart bleeds when it contemplates the fate of this noble people. What a melancholy picture of prostrate liberty is presented in the following paragraph:

"From the 3d to the 6th of March, the gates of Warsaw were closed, whilst arrests were made of the young Poles said to be implicated in the late insurrection, were sent to Riow, to be incorporated in the Russian regiments. A private letter states that those young men are sent off in tens of thousands to Siberia, to form colonies to people those dreary regions of perpetual snow and Cimmerian darkness. The pretended discovery of a new plot is the pretext for this wholesale banishment of the Polish race: including it is said not less than 40,000."

CHOLERA MORBUS

WE select an item under this head, which, gives an extensive view of this sweeping disease. The Atlantic cities tremble at the distant destruction of this irreconcilable foe to health and happiness, but the only alternative is, Trust in God. To endeavor to stay the progress of such a calamity by means, is-is what, why, what means would have stayed the angels' visit to the camp of the Assyrians?

The item is from the N. Y. Courier & Enquirer's Paris correspondent:

I find it impossible to procure the exact number of the deaths up to the latest moment with any pretensions to accuracy, but there cannot be the least doubt that they now exceed 10,000, and as the number of cases in the early stages of the disease when its character was more virulent than it has since become bore a proportion to the deaths somewhere between five to two and three to one, the number of persons effected by it may now be stated in round numbers to amount to at least 30,000 or about four per cent. on the whole mass of the population.

Supposing the disease to be suddenly arrested at its present point, which would be inconsistent with the whole of its previous history, the proportional loss which Paris has suffered with the other great cities of Europe which have yet been visited by the disease would be very considerable, as you will at once perceive on casting your eye over the following abstract, in which the 1st column gives the names of places, the second the amount of their population, the third the number of persons effected by the cholera and the fourth the number of deaths.

Moscow, ... 350,000 8,576 4,690

Petersburg, ... 360,000 9,247 4,757

Vienna, .. 300,000 3,980 1,899

Berlin, ... 240,000 2,220 1,401

Hamburgh, ... 100,000 874 455

Prague, ... 96,000 3,234 1,335

Breslaw, ... 78,000 1,276 670

Koenigsberg, ... 70,000 2,188 1,310

Magdebourg, ... 36,000 576 346

Braun, ... 33,000 1,540 604

Stettin, ... 24,000 366 250

Halle, ... 23,000 303 152

Elberg, ... 22,000 420 283

Hungary, ... 8,750,000 435,330 188,000

London, ... 1,500,000 2,534 1,328

Paris, ... 750,000 30,000 10,000

Edinburgh, ... 150,000 127 72

Glasgow, ... 180,000 782 395

Paisley, ... 60,000 359 204

HORRORS OF THE CHOLERA MORBUS.

We have witnessed in our days the birth of a new pestilence, which, in the short space of fourteen years, has desolated the fairest portion of the globe, and swept off at least fifty millions of our race. It has mastered every variety of climate, surmounted every natural barrier, conquered every people. It has not, like the simoon blasted life, and then passed away; the cholera, like small pox or plague, takes root in the soil which it has once possessed. The circumstances under which the individual is attacked are no less appalling than the history of the progress and mortality of the disease. In one man says an eye witness, the prostration of strength was so great the he could hardly move a limb, though he had been but fifteen minuits [minutes] before in service of an officer was seized in the act of picking up his rice, previous to going out to cut grass close to his master's feet, and being unable to call for assistance, he was observed by an other person at a distance from him, picking up small stones and pitching them towards him, for the purpose of attracting his notice. This man died in an hour. It is no wonder that the approach of such a pestilence has struck the deepest terror into every community.

The origin of this disease is not known. It broke out at Jessore, about a hundred miles south east of Calcutta, in August, 1817. "Spreading from village to village, and destroying thousands of the inhabitants, it reached Calcutta early in September. It then spread into other parts of the country, taking different places in succession; and at length it appeared in the grand army, and eventually extending over a large portion of Hindostan." In Bassora, which contained

60,000 inhabitants, in fourteen days it destroyed from 15,000 to 18,000 persons. In seven months, it had extended from Caramania to Judea, over a space of not less than a hundred leagues, and reached the shores of the Mediterranean. But it was introduced into Europe at the mouth of the Volga on the Caspian Sea, in 1830.-[London Quarterly Review.]

HYMNS

Selected and prepared for the Church of Christ, in these last days.

THE CELESTIAL HOME.

BEYOND these earthly scenes in sight, No curse those blissful regions know;

Immortal beings rest, In realms of infinite delight; Nor fears create despair,

The home of Jesus Christ. For sin, the source of every wo,

Can never enter there.

CHORUS. O the home, the glorious home, O the home, &c.

Of the beloved Son,

Where the righteous all shall meet There changing time is never known,

And be forever one! Nor Sun o'er mountain brow,

But God upon his shining throne

Celestial home! could our weak eyes Fills one eternal now.

But half its charms explore, O the home, &c.

How would our souls desire to rise,

And live on earth no more!

O the home, the glorious home, &c.

There pain and sorrow never come,

No; nothing there is vain;

But perfect peace, and ceaseless bloom,

With endless pleasure reign.

O the home, &c.

THE PILGRIMS' HYMNS

GO on, dear pilgrims, while below, Go on rejoicing day by day; Him, eye to eye, we there shall see

In wisdom's paths of peace, Your crown is yet before, Our face like his shall shine;

Determin'd nothing else to know, So fear no trials on the way, O! what a glorious company,

But Jesus' righteousness. The scene will soon be o'er. When saints and angels join!

Do like the Savior, follow him, Soon we shall reach the promis'd land, O! what a joyful meeting there,

He in this world has been, With all the ransom'd race In robes of white array!

And oft revil'd, but like a lamb, And meet with Enoch's perfect band, Palms in our hands we all shall bear,

Did ne'er revile again. To sing redeeming grace. And crowns that ne'er decay!

O take the pattern he has given, There we shall be when Christ appears, We'll hasten to our earthly home,

Seek first the things of worth, And all his glory see, While Jacob gathers in,

And learn the only way to heaven, And reign with him a thousand years, And watch our great Redeemer come,

Is-worship God on earth. When all the world is free. And make an end of sin.

Remember we must watch and pray Our souls are in his mighty hand, When we've been there a thousand years,

While journeying on the road, And he will keep them still; Bright shining as the Sun,

Lest we should fall out by the way If faithful, we shall surely stand We've no less days to sing God's praise,

And wound the cause of God. With him on Zion's hill. Than when we first begun.

BAD COMPANY, &c.

"EVIL communication," says the text, "corrupts good manners." The assertion is general, and no doubt all people suffer from such communication; but above all, the minds of youth will suffer; which are yet unformed, unprincipled, unfurnished, and ready to receive any impression.

But before we consider the danger of keeping bad company, let us first see the meaning of the phrase.

In the phrase of the world, good company means fashionable people. Their stations in life, not their morals are considered: and he, who associates with such, though they set him the example of breaking every commandment of the decalogue, is still said to keep good company. I should wish you to fix another meaning to the expression; and to consider vice in the same detestable light, in whatever company it is found; nay, to consider all company in which it is found, be their station what it will, as bad company.

The three following classes will perhaps include the greatest part of those, who deserve this appellation.

In the first, I should rank all who endeavor to destroy the principles of Christianity-who jest upon Scripture-talk blasphemy-and treat revelation with contempt.

A second class of bad company are those, who have a tendency to destroy in us the principles of common honesty and integrity. Under this head we may rank gamesters of every denomination; and low and infamous characters of every profession.

A third class of bad company, and such as are commonly most dangerous to youth, includes the long catalogue of men of pleasure. In whatever way they follow the call of appetite, they have equally a tendency to corrupt the purity of the mind.

Besides these three classes, whom we call bad company, there are others who come under the denomination of ill chosen company: trifling, insipid characters of every kind; who follow no business-are led by no ideas of improvement-but spend their time in disipation [dissipation] and folly-whose highest praise it is, that they are only not vicious-With none of these a serious man would wish his son to keep company.

It may be asked what is meant by keeping bad company? The world abounds with characters of this kind: they meet us in every place; and if we keep company at all, it is impossible to avoid keeping company with such persons.

It is true if we were determined never to have any commerce with bad men, we must, as the apostle remarks, "altogether go out of the world." By keeping bad company, therefore, is not meant a casual intercourse with them, on occasion of business, or as they accidentally fall in our way; but having an inclination to consort with them-complying with that inclination-seeking their company when we might avoid it-entering into their parties-and making them the companions of our choice. Mixing with them occasionally cannot be avoided.

The danger of keeping bad company, arises principally from our aptness to imitate and catch the manners and sentiments of others-from the power of custom-from our own bad inclinations-and from the pains taken by the bad to corrupt us.

In our earliest youth, the contagion of manners is observable. In the boy, yet incapable of having any thing instilled into him, we easily discover from his first actions, and rude attempts at language, the kind of persons with whom he has been brought up: we see the early spring of a civilized education, or the first wild shoots of rusticity.

As he enters farther into life, his behavior, manners, and conversation, all take their cast from the company he keeps. Observe the peasant, and the man of education; the difference is striking. And yet God hath bestowed equal talents on each. The only difference is, they have been thrown into different scenes of life; and have had commerce with persons of different stations.

Nor are manners and behavior more easily caught, than opinions and principles. In childhood and youth, we naturally adopt the sentiments of those about us.

And as we advance in life, how few of us think for ourselves; How many of us are satisfied with taking our opinions at second hand;

The great power and force of custom forms another argument against keeping bad company. However seriously disposed we may be; and however shocked at the first approaches of vice; this shocking appearance goes off upon an intimacy with it. Custom will soon render the most disgustful thing familiar. And this is indeed a kind provision of nature, to render labour [labor], and toil and danger, which are the lot of man, more easy to him.

The raw soldier who trembles at the first encounter becomes a hardy veteran in a few campaigns. Habit renders danger familiar, and of course indifferent to him.

But habit, which is intended for our good, may, like other kind appointments of nature, be converted into a mischief. The well-disposed youth, entering first into bad company, is shocked at what he hears, and what he sees. The good principles which he had imbibed, ring in his ears an alarming lesson against the wickedness of his companions. But alas! this sensibility is but of a day's continuance. The next jovial meeting makes the horrid picture of yesterday more easily endured.-[(->) To be continued.]

A correspondent of the Nat. Intelligencer, among the many preventives against the Cholera, says:-God will hear, if man will pray. This we endorse as truth.

Mental pleasures never cloy; unlike those of the body, they are increased by repetition, approved of by reflection, and strengthened by enjoyment.

A great man with the Lord, is what the world would call a poor wretch, or he is of no note. Thus the simple confound the wise.

The Evening and the Morning Star IS PUBLISHED EVERY MONTH AT INDEPENDENCE, JACKSON COUNTY, MO., BY W. W. PHELPS & CO. THE PRICE IS ONE DOLLAR FOR A YEAR IN ADVANCE, EXCEPT SPECIAL CONTRACTS WITH THE CHURCH.

EVERY PERSON THAT SENDS US $10, (U. S. PAPER,) SHALL BE ENTITLED TO A PAPER FOR A YEAR, GRATIS. ALL LETTERS TO THE EDITOR, OR PUBLISHERS, MUST BE POST PAID.

(->) ADVERTISEMENTS WILL BE INSERTED TO ORDER, IN THE ADVERTISER, AT THE USUAL RATES.

PRINTING, OF MOST KINDS, DONE TO ORDER, AND IN STYLE.

Made in the USA
Middletown, DE
14 March 2022

62628669R00057